Lecture Notes in Computer Science   **11317**

Commenced Publication in 1973
Founding and Former Series Editors:
Gerhard Goos, Juris Hartmanis, and Jan van Leeuwen

Editorial Board

More information about this series at http://www.springer.com/series/7408

Issa Traore · Isaac Woungang
Sherif Saad Ahmed · Yasir Malik (Eds.)

Intelligent, Secure, and Dependable Systems in Distributed and Cloud Environments

Second International Conference, ISDDC 2018
Vancouver, BC, Canada, November 28–30, 2018
Proceedings

Springer

Editors
Issa Traore (ID)
University of Victoria
Victoria, BC, Canada

Isaac Woungang (ID)
Ryerson University
Toronto, ON, Canada

Sherif Saad Ahmed
University of Windsor
Windsor, ON, Canada

Yasir Malik
Concordia University of Edmonton
Edmonton, AB, Canada

ISSN 0302-9743   ISSN 1611-3349 (electronic)
Lecture Notes in Computer Science
ISBN 978-3-030-03711-6   ISBN 978-3-030-03712-3   (eBook)
https://doi.org/10.1007/978-3-030-03712-3

Library of Congress Control Number: 2018960427

LNCS Sublibrary: SL2 – Programming and Software Engineering

This Springer imprint is published by the registered company Springer Nature Switzerland AG
The registered company address is: Gewerbestrasse 11, 6330 Cham, Switzerland

Welcome Message from ISDDC 2018 General Co-chairs

Welcome to the proceedings of the Second International Conference on Intelligent, Secure and Dependable Systems in Distributed and Cloud Environments (ISDDC 2018).

The past decade has witnessed tremendous advances in computing and networking technologies, with the appearance of new paradigms and the consolidation of existing ones. New paradigms such as the Internet of Things (IoT) and cloud computing and advances in mobile computation have disrupted how we live with, think of, interact with, and rely on computing technologies. Undoubtedly, the aforementioned technological advance helps improve many facets of human lives, for instance, through better health-care delivery, faster and more reliable communications, significant gains in productivity, and so on. At the same, it has raised significant challenges that we are still struggling to come to grips with effectively. Cybersecurity stands out as one of these areas that raise significant concerns about computing and networking technologies.

ISDDC is a conference series that provides a venue for researchers and practitioners to present, learn, and discuss recent advances in cybersecurity.

Every year, ISDDC receives several dozens of submissions from around the world. Building on the success from last year, ISDDC 2018 presented an exciting technical program that is the work of many volunteers. The program consisted of a combination technical papers, keynotes, and tutorials. The technical papers were peer reviewed by Program Committee (PC) members who are all cybersecurity experts and researchers, through a blind process.

We received a total of 28 papers this year, and accepted ten papers for inclusion in the proceedings and presentation at the conference, which corresponds to an acceptance rate of about 35%. Papers were reviewed by three PC members, in a single round of review.

ISDDC 2018 was also privileged to have select guest speakers to provide stimulating presentations on topics of wide interest. This year's distinguished speakers were:

- Dr. Baljeet Malhotra, Director of Research at Synopsys Inc., and Founder of TeejLab Inc.
- Mr. Deepak Rout, Executive Cybersecurity Advisor, Microsoft Inc.
- Mr. Mustapha Rachidi, Security Analyst, Bulletproof

We would like to thank all of the volunteers for their contributions to ISDDC 2018. Our thanks go to the authors, and our sincere gratitude goes to the Program Committee, who gave much extra time to carefully review the submissions.

We are pleased to announce selected papers will be invited to submit extended versions for publication in the Wiley journal *Security and Privacy*.

We would also like to thank the local organizing team, in particular Dean Irene Young and Ms. Lee Harris, from New York Institute of Technology, for their support and hard work in making this event a success. Our thanks go to our sponsors:

- New York Institute of Technology Vancouver Campus, for hosting ISDDC 2018
- Springer, for publishing the conference proceedings

Finally, we thank all the attendees and the larger ISDDC community for their continuing support, by submitting papers and by volunteering their time and talent in other ways.

We hope you will find the papers in the proceedings interesting.

Issa Traore
Isaac Woungang

Welcome Message from ISDDC 2018 Program Co-chairs

Welcome to the proceedings of the Second International Conference on Intelligent, Secure and Dependable Systems in Distributed and Cloud Environments (ISDDC 2018), which was held during November 28–30, at the New York Institute of Technology (NYIT), Vancouver, BC, Canada.

ISDDC provides a forum for cybersecurity researchers and practitioners from industry and government to meet and exchange ideas about progress and advances in the emerging areas of intelligent, secure, dependable systems and cloud environments.

The papers selected for publication in the proceedings of ISDDC 2018 span many research issues related to the design, analysis, implementation, management and control of dependable and secure systems, and covering aspects such as algorithms, architectures, and protocols dealing with network computing, ubiquitous and cloud systems, and Internet of Things systems. Operational security, intrusion detection, biometrics, cyber-threat intelligence, blockchain technology, access control and secure task offloading/storage in cloud computing, multiparty trust negotiation over distributed systems, to name a few, are examples of areas and applications of these contributed papers. We hope the participants of this conference will benefit from this coverage of a wide range of current hot-spot security-related topics.

In this edition, 28 papers were submitted, and peer-reviewed by the Program Committee members and external reviewers who are experts in the topical areas covered by the papers. The Program Committee accepted ten papers (about 35% acceptance ratio).

The conference program also included two distinguished keynote speeches and two tutorials.

Our thanks go to the many volunteers who contributed to the organization of ISDDC 2018. We would like to thank all authors for submitting their papers. We would also like to thank the Program Committee members for thoroughly reviewing the submissions and making valuable recommendations. We would like to thank the ISDDC 2018 local arrangements team for the excellent organization of the conference, and for their effective coordination creating the recipe for a very successful conference.

We hope you will enjoy the conference proceedings.

October 2018

Yasir Malik
Sherif Saad Ahmed

Organization

ISDCC 2018 Organizing Committee

General Co-chairs

Issa Traore   University of Victoria, Canada
Isaac Woungang   Ryerson University, Canada

Publicity Co-chairs

Isaac Woungang   Ryerson University, Canada
Watheq Elkarachi   Ain Shams University, Egypt

Program Co-chairs

Yasir Malik   Concordia University, Canada
Sherif Saad Ahmed   University of Windsor, Canada

Local Arrangements Chairs

Ahmed Awad   University of Washington, Bothell, USA
Tokunbo Makanju   New York Institute of Technology, Vancouver, Canada

Tutorial Chair

Ahmed Awad   University of Washington, Bothell, USA

Technical Program Committee

Petros Nicopolitidis   Aristotle University of Thessaloniki, Greece
Ilsun You   Soonchunhyang University, Republic of Korea
Wei Lu   Keene State College, USA
Sherali Zeadally   University of Kentucky, USA
Luca Caviglione   CNIT, Italy
Reza M. Parizi   New York Institute of Technology, Nanjing, China
Hamed Aly   Acadia University, Canada
Christine Chan   University of Regina, Canada
Enrico Schiavone   University of Florence, Italy
Rohit Ranchal   IBM Watson Health Cloud, USA
Danda B. Rawat   Howard University, USA

Marcelo Luis Brocardo	University of Santa Catarina, Brazil
Mohammad Derawi	Norwegian University of Science and Technology, Norway
Yudong Liu	Western Washington University, Bellingham, WA, USA
Babak Beheshti	New York Institute of Technology, New York, NY, USA
Wenjia Li	New York Institute of Technology, New York, NY, USA
Ahmed Mousaad	IBM Watson, USA
Ahmed Mostafa	Microsoft Amsterdam Area, The Netherlands
Watheq Elkarachi	Ain Shams University, Egypt
Isaac Woungang	Ryerson University, Canada
Issa Traore	University of Victoria, Canada
Sherif Saad Ahmed	University of Windsor, Canada
Yasir Malik	Concordia University of Edmonton, Canada
Ahmed Awad	University of Washington, Bothell, USA
Tokunbo Makanju	New York Institute of Technology, Vancouver, Canada
Amin Milani Fard	New York Institute of Technology, Vancouver, Canada
Wei Li	Northern Illinois University, DeKalb, USA

ISDDC 2018 Keynote Talks

Data-Driven Intelligence for Security Vulnerability Management at Scale

Baljeet Malhotra

Director of Research at Synopsys Inc., and Founder of TeejLab Inc.

Abstract. Monitoring publicly known security vulnerabilities in software systems is very important for enterprises. Organizations such as National Institute of Standards and Technology (NIST) regularly publish vulnerability reports (using Common Vulnerability Enumeration or CVE) to secure national IT networks and protect business interests at large. The main challenge in this context is that the software systems or tools against which the vulnerabilities are published are typically known differently to various stake holders that consume those vulnerable software systems. For instance, an organization may refer to one of its software components as my.program.js, however NIST may report a vulnerability on that particular software component as org_program.js according to their standards (using Common Platform Enumeration or CPE). Thousands of vulnerabilities are reported against millions of software components every year, which makes this problem very complex. In this talk, we'll discuss about a system that we built to match imprecise pieces of unstructured data to track vulnerabilities in software systems. The heart of the system is Natural Language Processing techniques that are capable of searching vulnerabilities from large volumes of unstructured data regardless of how the software systems are named. We'll conclude with a view on data-driven intelligence that can address the scalability and volume issues faced by commercial vulnerability management solutions.

Incident Management:
Investigating a Malware

Mustapha Rachidi

Security Analyst at Bulletproof, Fredericton, New Brunswick

Abstract. Security Analyst is a challenging role in performing a good investigation of all security incidents that occur. On that account, the role demands continuous monitoring to make sure the environment is always healthy and secure. For that reason, Security Analysts use lots of tools and technologies like Security Information and Event Management (SIEM) that provides real-time analysis of security logs and events generated by applications and network appliances. A good resolution of any incident requires us to have an incident management process put in place with well defined procedures that detail the appropriate responses to incidents. The objective of having such a process is to restore the operations back to normal when an incident occurs while minimizing the risk by limiting the incident impact. In this presentation, the different phases of an incident management process will be explained from a security analyst perspective. Then, in this presentation, a real application for the incident management process will be discussed: a malware that has been detected will be investigated while following the process of the incident response management that is used by the SOC to mitigate the impact, analyze the malware and make the necessary response to restore the operations to normal.

Cyber Resiliency in the Era of Cloud, Mobility and Big Data

Deepak Rout

Executive Security Advisor, Microsoft Canada

Abstract. Digital transformation is revolutionizing our world. Cloud computing, Social Media, and Mobile technologies have re-modelled our world, and are being further reshaped at a rapid pace by Artificial Intelligence and Machine Learning paradigms. This has created an unprecedented impact globally across both enterprises and consumers, posing significant risks that needs to be acknowledged and managed. It is important to know how your business or organization is impacted by cyber resiliency and further, how you can help your business addressing such issue. Partnership with organizations with unique insights into cloud, mobility and artificial intelligence may go a long way in this regard. The objective of this talk is to share some light on how to deal with the issue of cyber resiliency in this Era of cloud, mobility and Bigdata.

ISDDC 2018 Tutorials

Attack Graphs in Cybersecurity – Evolution and Practice

Paulo Quinan

University of Victoria, ECE Department, Victoria, BC, Canada

Abstract. Attack Graphs are very powerful tools used in many areas of information security including threat modelling, intrusion detection and prevention and forensic analysis given their capabilities in helping security analysts identify how attackers can exploit, or have exploited, vulnerabilities in a system in order to compromise it. Traditionally, attack graphs were generated manually, however that is an error prone process that gets exponentially harder the more elements or nodes are added to the system being analyzed. To overcome this issue many automatic generation tools and techniques have been proposed, and while those tools have allowed the generation of attack graphs of very large and complex systems, they have also made the analysis of the resulting attack graphs ever more complex. That is compounded by the ever growing number of attack graph variations, each aiming to elucidate different aspects of the security issues faced by the system. Together, the complexity and the large number of variations used in the industry, mean that learning to generate and analyze attack graphs can be a daunting task even for experienced security analysts. This tutorial aims to help those wishing to start learning about attack graphs by presenting an introductory overview of the subject. We will discuss how and when to use them, some of their most common types, like the state attack graph, the logical attack graph, the privilege graph and the vulnerability graph, the different tools and techniques used to generate them, and some of the most important open challenges in the field.

Engineering Location Privacy Attacks in VANETs

Ikjot Saini

School of Computer Science, University of Windsor, Windsor, ON, Canada

Abstract. Vehicular Ad-hoc Networks (VANET) are envisioned as an integral part of Intelligent Transportation Systems. However, the security and privacy risks associated with the wireless communication are often overlooked. In fact, messages exchanged in VANET wireless communication carries personally identifiable information. This introduces several privacy threats that could limit the adaptation of VANET.PREXT is a unified and extensible framework that simulate pseudonym change schemes (i.e. privacy schemes) in VANET. It supports seven privacy schemes of different approaches including silent period, context-based and mix-zone and can be easily extended to include more schemes. It includes adversary modules that can eavesdrop vehicle messages and track their movements. This adversary is used in measuring the gained privacy in terms of several popular metrics such as entropy, traceability, and pseudonym usage statistics. In this short Tutorial, we will demonstrate how location privacy attacks could be designed, implemented and analyzed using PREXT and other VANETs simulations tools.

Static Analysis in Fileless Cryptocurrency-mining Malware

Liu Meijia

AV Analyst, Fortinet Inc., Vancouver, BC, Canada

Abstract. Fileless Malware attacks became dramatically increasing since 2016. It is well known that antivirus software is designed to scan computers by malware signatures and block thesemalware from executing. Unlike traditional malware intends to trick people to download files or exploit software flaw to install files for delivering payload, fileless malware executes malicious code directly from memory rather than installing any software on a target machine. Since there are no malware files on the hard disk, it is more difficult to detect. The mining fileless malware that this tutorial provided utilize legitimate software tools like Windows Management Instrumentation (WMI) and PowerShell to infect machines by obfuscated script. The PowerShell script is executed to communicate with C&C server and update to the latest version. By Mimikatz tool, the user account details from the infected machine are obtained in the process. It can propagate itself via WMI and EternalBlue, and place itself into remote computer WMI database. Furthermore, it exploits vulnerabilities in MS16-032, MS15-051 and CVE-2018-8120 to escalate user privileges depending on 32-bit and 64-bit operating system. At last, it uses WMI as persistence mechanism to launch miner with the reflective PE injection about every 93.3 minutes. Finally, the tutorial is offering some countermeasures to avoid this kind of attack. According to today's threat in cybersecurity, scanning the hard drive for malicious files is not enough for antivirus team. Looking for evidence in memory becomes indispensable part during antivirus work.

Contents

Identifying Vulnerabilities and Attacking Capabilities Against Pseudonym
Changing Schemes in VANET 1
    Ikjot Saini, Sherif Saad, and Arunita Jaekel

An RSA-Based User Authentication Scheme for Smart-Homes
Using Smart Card 16
    *Maninder Singh Raniyal, Isaac Woungang,
    and Sanjay Kumar Dhurandher*

Analysing Data Security Requirements of Android Mobile
Banking Application 30
    Shikhar Bhatnagar, Yasir Malik, and Sergey Butakov

Adaptive Mobile Keystroke Dynamic Authentication Using Ensemble
Classification Methods. 38
    Faisal Alshanketi, Issa Traoré, Awos Kanan, and Ahmed Awad

Automating Incident Classification Using Sentiment Analysis
and Machine Learning 50
    Marina Danchovsky Ibrishimova and Kin Fun Li

Security Analysis of an Identity-Based Data Aggregation Protocol
for the Smart Grid. 63
    Zhiwei Wang, Hao Xie, and Yumin Xu

A More Efficient Secure Fully Verifiable Delegation Scheme
for Simultaneous Group Exponentiations 74
    Stephan Moritz and Osmanbey Uzunkol

An Efficient Framework for Improved Task Offloading
in Edge Computing 94
    Amanjot Kaur and Ramandeep Kaur

Secure and Efficient Enhanced Sharing of Data Over Cloud Using Attribute
Based Encryption with Hash Functions 102
    Prabhleen Singh and Kulwinder Kaur

Blockchain Technology and Its Applications in FinTech 118
    Wei Lu

Author Index 125

Contents

Identifying Vulnerabilities and Attacking Capabilities Against Pseudonym Changing Schemes in VANET

Ikjot Saini, Sherif Saad$^{(\boxtimes)}$, and Arunita Jaekel

School of Computer Science, University of Windsor, Windsor, Canada
{saini11s,shsaad,arunita}@uwindsor.ca

Abstract. Vehicular communication discloses critical information about the vehicle. Association of this information to the drivers put the privacy of the driver at risk. The broadcast of safety messages in plain text is essential for safety applications but not secure with respect to the privacy of the driver. Many pseudonymous schemes are proposed in the literature, yet the level of privacy is not being compared among these schemes. Our contribution in this paper is the identification of the vulnerabilities in the existing pseudonym changing schemes, determining the attacking capabilities of the local-passive attacker and demonstration of the optimal case for an attacker to deploy the network of eavesdropping stations with the feasible attacking capabilities. We have also provided the analysis and comparison of the different pseudonym changing schemes with a new metric to measure tracking ability of the local-passive attacker in highway and urban scenarios as well as with the varying number of attacking stations.

Keywords: Vehicular Ad Hoc Networks · Pseudonym
Location privacy · Tracking

1 Introduction

One of the open challenges in Vehicular Ad-hoc Networks (VANETs) is the protection of location privacy and personally identifiable information that could be collected from Basic Safety Messages (BSM). The safety messages play an important role in safety applications in VANETs. Vehicular networks are expected to improve road safety by preventing potential accidents and significantly enhance traffic management. VANETs safety applications aim to provide the awareness of the surroundings of the vehicle such as information of neighboring vehicles which helps in avoiding the potential collisions in real time. The safety applications use a dedicated set of messages tailored for localized and low latency broadcast for vehicle to vehicle communication. These safety messages are known as Basic Safety Messages. A typical BSM message contains information about the vehicle's current state such as position, speed, heading and other sensors information

© Springer Nature Switzerland AG 2018
I. Traore et al. (Eds.): ISDDC 2018, LNCS 11317, pp. 1–15, 2018.
https://doi.org/10.1007/978-3-030-03712-3_1

required for the safety applications. For the safety reasons, this message beaconing is broadcast 10 times per second. Also, the information is not encrypted due to the real time transmission which makes this information vulnerable to various privacy and security attacks. The safety messages can be received by anyone in vehicle's communication range of 300 m. This enables the traceability of the vehicle as the vehicle is leaving a trail of location updates along with information. These mobility traces can be linked to the personal information of the driver. The risk associated with the information disclosure elevates when continuous stream of BSMs are eavesdropped for longer time period. For example, by collecting and analyzing traffic patterns it can reveal the frequently visited places such as home and work [1]. Collecting this information over long duration could enable profiling drivers and maybe collecting personal information such as name, work address, home address, and regular daily activities. This is of course poses many privacy and security risks. Therefore, it is necessary to find the balance between broadcasting safety application data such as BSM and to protect the privacy of the driver and vehicles.

Not only the information disclosure is the problem but also the authentication of these messages is very important as the manipulated, false, or forged messages could cause many safety problems. The proposed solution for the authentication problem is using cryptographic temporary identifiers that replace other permanent vehicle identifiers such as Vehicle Identification Number (VIN). These temporary identifiers are called pseudonyms [2]. Currently, pseudonyms are the part of the emerging standards for the vehicle to vehicle communication. According to the U.S. Department of Transportation (USDOT), the Security Management Credential System (SCMS) is the Proof-of-concept message security solution for the vehicular communications [3]. Pseudonyms have limited lifetime and are used for the authentication without revealing the original personal information of the vehicle such as vehicle identifier. Every vehicle in the network is given a set of pseudonyms which can be used over a period of three years. In emerging standards [4], it has been proposed that these pseudonyms must be used in a specific manner so that the number of pseudonyms does not exhaust due to frequent changes. Therefore, it is proposed that only 20 pseudonyms are usable for a week. This pseudonym issuance ensures that the pseudonyms are not needed to be refilled up to three years.

Pseudonyms may have resolved the problem of the authentication of safety message, but this temporary identifier is still having ability to link the location updates of the moving vehicle if the temporary identifier remains for a long time in the network. Hence, the mobility tracing can be prevented using an individual pseudonym for only a certain time during the trip and changing the pseudonyms frequently in a longer trip. In the last decade, a number of pseudonym changing schemes has been proposed. These schemes have different location privacy metrics and techniques. However, the effectiveness of these schemes has not been evaluated against the location privacy attacks in different traffic scenarios such as urban, highway, or rural. It is important to determine which pseudonym changing scheme is applicable to what kind of traffic scenario. Another very important aspect is the attacking capabilities of the attacker. Mainly, there are two types of attacks which are local and global passive attacks. In the global passive attack, the Road Side Units (RSUs) are used as the attacking stations and the attacker can listen to the safety message either by taking control over the widespread network of the RSUs or by deploying a significant number of listening stations. While in a local passive attack, the attacker places the listening stations in a limited area. Considering the high cost of the equipment, the local adversary tries to minimize the number of attacking stations while having maximum coverage in the potential areas where vehicles tend to change their pseudonyms. The feasibility of the global attacking scenario diminishes as the attacker either has to control a number of RSUs or place very costly equipment, however, it cannot be said that it is unrealistic. On the other hand, the local adversary is achievable with a fewer number of attacking stations placed strategically based on the knowledge of the pseudonym changing scheme as well as the preliminary traffic analysis. The major privacy issue arises when there is a global passive attacker as it can listen to a continuous stream of beacons which updates the location, direction, and speed. Even though the vehicle changes the pseudonym, the spatiotemporal information helps in identifying the vehicle by correlating the pseudonyms. But in the case of the local attacker, the vehicles may not encounter any eavesdropping station or the number of deployed listening stations are very few which cannot correlate the pseudonyms after a certain time. The limited capabilities of the local passive attacker reduce the vehicle tracking.

In this paper, we have discussed the effectiveness of the existing pseudonym changing schemes and have analyzed the impact of the schemes on the location privacy in the presence of local passive adversaries and provided the comparison of the traceability and frequency of pseudonym change. For local attacker in urban and highway scenarios, we analyzed the effect of the varying number of eavesdropping stations on the different pseudonym changing schemes. As the deployment of a large number of eavesdropping stations is not feasible due to the high cost, the attacker would aim to use a minimum number of eavesdropping stations with maximum coverage. We considered the best case for the attacker in our simulation with maximum possible listening ability. A vehicle is considered to be successfully tracked only when the attacker correctly identifies the vehicle based on the association of pseudonyms and spatiotemporal information. Traceability is based on the number of vehicles correctly tracked and the total number of vehicles in the scenario. Another factor is the frequency of the pseudonym change that highly affects the driver's location privacy and the performance of the pseudonym changing scheme. Many of the schemes do not consider the frequency and it has not been clearly discussed in the development of various pseudonym changing schemes. Having a limited number of pseudonyms for a certain time forces the vehicles to reuse the pseudonyms. Repetition of the temporary identifier is not a good idea as it is associated with a certain vehicle and reuse of the pseudonym ease the correlation between the old and new pseudonyms of the same vehicle.

2   Background

There is a number of research papers which discuss the change of the pseudonyms and these proposed schemes are either based on the dynamic change or fixed change of the pseudonyms. The dynamic pseudonym change is based on the various factors like vehicular density trigger [5], speed-based trigger [6], or random encryption periods [7]. All these changes can only be determined when a certain event takes place. Hence, these schemes have relatively more privacy protection as the local passive attacker may not know when the vehicles would change the pseudonyms. On the other hand, there are fixed pseudonym changing schemes which allow the pre-determination of the pseudonym changes as these schemes repeat a pattern which can be deduced over a certain duration of tracking. The mix zone based [8] and time slot-based [9] pseudonym changing schemes have fixed pseudonym changes based on the area and time, respectively. However, these schemes are more predictable as these involve a certain pattern for changing the pseudonyms. The time slot based is the common approach in which the pseudonyms are changed after a fixed time duration. One of such schemes is currently the part of the emerging standards. According to the proposed standards [4], every vehicle will use a set of 20 pseudonyms for a week and after every 5 min, the pseudonym will be changed. The problem with this scheme is the repetition of the pseudonyms after the usage of all 20 pseudonyms over the week. Many schemes have proposed the radio silence [10] during the pseudonym change to disconnect the continuous listening of the safety messages by passive attacker. This may provide the optimal solution for the privacy protection but it compromises the safety because many of the safety messages will not be transmitted due to radio silence. There are a number of limitations of the pseudonym changes and it is important to evaluate the effectiveness of such schemes on the basis of location privacy, attacking capabilities, realistic traffic scenarios, safety and efficiency.

Pseudonym changes have been evaluated in several works, however, each of these has different perspective for the evaluation. Most of the simulations are done using the simplistic traffic scenario. Troncoso et al. [11] have shown that the re usability of the pseudonym affects the privacy and must be avoided. The simulation for this is performed on the Manhattan grid scenario. Wiedersheim et al. [12] demonstrated that the high frequency rate of the safety message discloses the relation of old and new pseudonyms as these become easy to resolve. Pan et al. [5] has proposed the cooperative scheme in which the pseudonyms are changed according to a trigger based on neighboring vehicles. If a vehicle needs to change the pseudonym and it comes in contact with a certain number of vehicles, it requests for the simultaneous pseudonym change and these vehicles change the pseudonyms together. Emara et al. [13] showed that user privacy preferences are also required to consider while changing the pseudonyms as the vehicle may pass through sensitive areas or in sparse vehicular network where there are not enough vehicles to reach the threshold for changing pseudonyms. Therefore, context-aware schemes determine the most suitable time to change the pseudonym with a very short radio silence time that does not affect the safety applications. We observed that the pseudonym changes based on cooperative [5] and context-aware [13] schemes are more efficient and better in terms of providing privacy protection.

3 Privacy Vulnerabilities

There are a number of vulnerabilities in the existing pseudonym changing schemes which compromise the privacy of the driver.

3.1 Linking Ability of Location Updates

Pseudonyms may have resolved the problem of the authentication of safety message, but this temporary identifier is still having ability to link the location updates of the moving vehicle if the temporary identifier remains for a long time in the network. Even though the vehicle changes the pseudonym, the spatiotemporal information helps in identifying the vehicle by correlating the pseudonyms. Hence, the mobility tracing can be prevented using an individual pseudonym for only a certain time during the trip and changing the pseudonyms frequently in a longer trip. In the last decade, a number of PCS has been proposed. These schemes have different location privacy metrics and techniques. However, the effectiveness of these schemes has not been evaluated against the location privacy attacks in different traffic scenarios such as urban, highway, or rural. It is important to determine which pseudonym changing scheme is applicable to what kind of traffic scenario.

3.2 Frequency of Pseudonym Change

The pseudonyms are required to change within a time duration so that a longer eavesdropping session does not disclose the information associated with a complete trip. If this happens more often, then the attacker can deduce the frequently visited places by a vehicle and therefore, can profile the driver based on the mobility patterns and routine activities. Hence, it is important that the vehicles change the pseudonym often so that attacker can not track complete trips. On the other hand, some existing pseudonym schemes allow the pseudonyms to change at a very high rate. This condition is suitable with respect to privacy but it arises problem with the issuance and re-issuance of the pseudonyms as every vehicle has limited number of pseudonyms.

3.3 Affect of Repetition

Many of PCS uses a large number of pseudonyms as the changing frequency is higher. It is not practical to use such a large number of pseudonyms. The issuance of these temporary identifiers is also one of the major concern. It has been suggested [4] that in initial phase, the set of pseudonyms issued to the vehicle must be valid for 3 years. Therefore, there is a limited number of pseudonyms. If used with higher frequency, then the vehicle will exhaust all the pseudonyms relatively sooner. Once the vehicle has used all the pseudonyms, it has to repeat as new set of pseudonyms will be issued after 3 years. The repetition is a privacy concern because the attacker records all the pseudonyms associated with a vehicle and repetition increases the tracking success. According to [4], 20 pseudonyms are active for a week and with the changing frequency of 5 min, all 20 pseudonyms will be in knowledge of the attacker in continuous 100 min of eavesdropping.

3.4   Knowledge of Pseudonym Changing Scheme

The attackers can take advantage by having the information of PCS used by the vehicles. This knowledge benefits the attacker in the placement of the equipment. If all the vehicles are following same scheme in all the scenarios, various factors like traffic congestion, fixed time interval for the change and intersection mix zones helps the attacker to decide the most suitable location for placement for maximum coverage.

4   Attacking Capabilities

There are different capabilities of the attacker which are important to consider while assessing the location privacy provided by the pseudonym changing schemes. Mainly, there are two types of attacks which are local and global passive attacks.

4.1   Feasibility of Global Passive Attack

In the global passive attack, the Road Side Units (RSUs) are used as the attacking stations and the attacker can listen to the safety message either by taking control over the widespread network of the RSUs or by deploying a significant number of listening stations. The feasibility of the global attacking scenario reduces as the attacker either has to control a number of RSUs or place very costly equipment, however, it cannot be said that it is unrealistic. The major privacy issue arises when global passive attacker is present as it can listen to continuous stream of beacons which updates the location, direction and speed.

4.2   Achievable Local Passive Attack

While in a local passive attack, the attacker places the listening stations in a limited area. Considering the high cost of the equipment, the local adversary tries to minimize the number of attacking stations while having maximum coverage in the potential areas where vehicles tend to change their pseudonyms. The local adversary is achievable with a fewer number of attacking stations placed strategically based on the knowledge of the pseudonym changing scheme as well as the preliminary traffic analysis. The vehicles may not encounter any eavesdropping station or the number of deployed listening stations are very few which cannot correlate the pseudonyms after certain time. The limited capabilities of the local passive attacker reduce the vehicle tracking with respect to global passive attack.

4.3   Communication Range

The equipment for the eavesdropping is more likely to be a Roadside Unit (RSU) deployed by the attacker. The communication range of a typical RSU varies from 100 to 1000 m. Smaller communication range provides highly reliable channel without dropping packets while longer range results in packet drop due to obstacle shadowing. The communication range of 300 m is considered reliable with the least packet drop ratio. Clearly, the longer communication range allows eavesdropping of more number of vehicles. Therefore, the attacker intends to use to communication range which does not drop any packet as well as can cover maximum area.

4.4   Equipment Placement

Strategically placing the equipment is a significant step for an attacker as it is the source of all the inferable information and he would like to collect as much information as possible. In order to achieve this, the attacker needs to know the type of PCS being used. Once he has the knowledge of PCS, he can estimate the potential attacking points based on preliminary traffic analysis, distance and frequency of pseudonym change. The placement for urban scenario is more likely to be different from highways. The tracking success is highly dependent on the placement of adversaries.

4.5   Number of Equipment

As the attacker may not have a large number of attacking equipment, therefore, the optimal solution for the attacker would be to use minimum number of equipment with maximum communication range. Preliminary traffic analysis helps the attacker to optimize the selection of eavesdropping area with respect to available number of equipment.

4.6   Longer Eavesdropping

The collection of the information by an eavesdropper is more useful when the vehicles are in range of the attacker for longer duration. Therefore, it is also an essential consideration for the attacker that the target vehicle remains in the network of the attacking equipment for continuous eavesdropping. The longer tracking allows the attacker to gain the knowledge of maximum possible number of pseudonyms, visited places and chosen routes. In case, PCS with high frequency of pseudonym change allows the repetition of the pseudonyms, then the attacker can identify the vehicle without any effort.

5   Simulation Setup

We have performed the simulation using OMNET++ [16], version 5.3 and Simulation of Urban MO-bility (SUMO) [15]; it is a discrete event simulator for the networks which simulate based on the components and modules. To connect OMNET++ with SUMO, we have used the extension Veins [17]. It is a vehicular network simulation framework. Further, PREXT is the privacy extension for the simulation of privacy schemes. It allows to analyze different pseudonym changing schemes within the same observation framework. Therefore, the privacy of a variety of schemes can be compared against each other based on the same privacy metric. Our goal is to evaluate and compare the privacy provided by different PCS in two very different scenarios. The network for the vehicles is not similar to other wireless networks. Therefore, we have used a specific mobility model for the vehicular network in our experiments. Also, the attacker has different capabilities, therefore, in the experiments, we have followed an attacker model which specifies the extent of the attacker's capabilities to eavesdrop.

5.1   Mobility Model

The mobility model describes the movement of the vehicles in the network. The macroscopic mobility features depend on road network which comprises length of the road, number of intersections, number of lanes, directional information of the road. While on a microscopic level, the features are included as speed of the driver, acceleration, traffic signs and other vehicles. Many of these parameters can be altered to simulate the required traffic scenario. Mobility models closer to reality produce more realistic simulations and results. For our experimental setup, we have used Simulation of Urban MO-bility (SUMO) which provides the support to the real map files from the OpenStreetMap [18]. For the evaluation in urban areas and highways, we have considered separate traffic scenarios which are large enough to simulate longer trips of the vehicles over 2–8 h. SUMO allows to simulate realistic synthetic traffic. The trips in the urban scenario are random which means that the vehicles are traveling from different starting points to destination points. While in the highway scenario, the vehicles are bound to follow a route but different vehicles have different entry and ending points. The urban scenario is more populated than the highway. The time durations for the evaluation, in Table 1, are different for urban and highway because in the city, the vehicles have average of 1 to 3 h trip but the highway may have longer trips ranging from 3 to 6 h. Therefore, the highway scenario is evaluated for relatively longer duration that is 6 h. We considered maximum time period in both scenarios for our work. To have simplified simulation scenario and evaluate the maximum capabilities of the attacker, we have considered that there is the least obstacle shadowing. While the radio transmission in real world gets heavily affected by the signal shadowing effect in urban areas due to buildings and other vehicles on the road which block radio propagation. In our simulation, we used simple obstacle shadowing which benefits the eavesdropper and allows the transmission of all the safety messages to the eavesdropper without significant packet loss.

5.2   Attacker Model

Our observation focuses on the aspects of the attacker in local passive attacking scenario. For local adversary, we have considered that the attacking stations are placed strategically so that the attacker can take advantage of the dense traffic and frequently chosen routes which are usually in the center of the city. The limited capabilities of the attacker may affect in the urban areas differently than the highways. Also, the local attacks are targeted to the busy areas within the city as attacker wants to use minimum number of attacking stations to reduce the overall cost. So we have simulated the local attack with varying number of attacking stations for different pseudonym changing schemes. It not only reveals the attacking capabilities but also shows the level of privacy protection provided by different schemes. For our work, we have considered that the safety messages are not encrypted. PREXT provides a unified framework for the simulation of the pseudonym changing schemes which aim to provide privacy in vehicular networks. It also involves the attacking modules which passively listen to the safety messages sent by vehicles. We have altered the attacking capabilities in this framework. We have placed the listening stations at the selected observation points based on preliminary traffic analysis. All the listening stations placed at different locations collect messages and send to a central tracker where the attacker determines the relation of the old and new pseudonyms used by same vehicle [14]. The attacker is not able to receive all the messages from the vehicles as one eavesdropping station covers limited area, hence, when the vehicles are in the range of one of the attacking station and change the pseudonym, then the attacker can directly correlate the changed pseudonym. The tracker also has capability of estimating based on the spatial-temporal relation. As the vehicle moves on a road and in a certain direction at a time, the speed of the vehicle helps in estimating the movement of the vehicle in given time which allows to determine that it is the same vehicle which previously had a pseudonym P1 and when it enters in the range of the new attacking station, it has new pseudonym P2. This correlation of the pseudonyms is observable only because of the continuous Basic Safety Messages and the smaller changing frequency of the pseudonyms. There are various factors which strengthen the attacking capabilities of the eavesdropper as discussed in Sect. 4. First of all, the attacker's communication range has direct impact on the accuracy and successful tracking probability of the attacker. We kept the 300 m of the range. Secondly, the knowledge of the pseudonym changing scheme has direct effect on the attacker's capabilities. This information allows the attacker to determine the placements of the listening stations.

The placement of the attacking station is an important consideration. Some of the places are the center of the city, highly dense areas, intersection of main routes within the city and most visited places within the city. We placed the attacking station strategically with consideration that most of the vehicular trips are made through that area. The urban scenario differs from the highways as the probability of changing routes and direction are higher in the city area while on the highways, the vehicles move usually follows a certain pattern. The vehicles are bound to go in one direction for certain distance unless there is an exit and the highways have speed limits as well. Both of these factors introduce vulnerabilities which are taken into account for the attacking capabilities in our model. The listening stations are placed based on the minimum distance covered by the vehicle before changing pseudonym based on the periodical pseudonym changing scheme. We considered this placement because the fixed pseudonym changing schemes allow predicting the precise position where the vehicle tends to change the pseudonym based on the allowable speed and predefined time for pseudonym change. Such placements are more realistic when different vehicular trips at different time are generated. This traffic scenario will allow to estimating the minimum number of attacking stations needed to have potential strong tracking within a limited area. When a message is received by the eavesdropping station then it is checked if the beacon is complete. In case, the message is not completely received then the message is discarded and it is not recorded by the eavesdropper.

5.3   Observed Pseudonym Changing Schemes

We have selected four of the pseudonym changing schemes for the analysis and comparison of the privacy. These are different from each other and do not follow the same techniques for pseudonym change.

Periodical Scheme. Brecht et al. [4] proposed the periodical changing scheme for the pseudonyms and it is going to be the part of the emerging standards in North America. This scheme is based on the limitation of the pseudonym usage so that the given pool of pseudonyms can be used for three years. The vehicle is given twenty pseudonyms for a week and every five minutes, the pseudonym is changed when the vehicle is active.

SLOW. Buttyan et al. [6] proposed the scheme based on the speed trigger. When the speed of the vehicle drops down 30 Km/hr then the pseudonym is changed. It is the user centric and dynamic scheme in which the vehicle changes the pseudonym without determining the fixed area or periodic change. Therefore, the timing of the pseudonym change would be relatively randomized than the periodical changing scheme.

Cooperative. In the cooperative scheme [5], the vehicle changes the pseudonym when there is at least one of the other vehicle which wants to change the pseudonym. This creates the confusion for the attacker which is more effective in the dense traffic scenarios in which the vehicles are closer to each other and the changed pseudonym of the vehicle cannot be resolved or correlated by the attacker.

Context-Aware Scheme. CAPS [13] is the context-aware scheme that let the vehicle decide when to change the pseudonym with a limited time of radio silence.

The radio silence is arguably not ideal for the safety messages but this scheme provides a better compromise between traceability and Quality of Service than a random silent period scheme.

6 Evaluation

We have simulated the highway and urban scenarios with realistic synthetic traffic generated by SUMO. The trips in the urban scenario are random which means that the vehicles are traveling from different starting points to destination points in both the scenarios. Vehicles join the network at different simulation time which means not all the vehicles are present at the beginning and the end of the simulation. In the highway scenario, the vehicles are bound to follow a route but different vehicles have different entry and ending points. The urban scenario is more populated than the highway and has more complexity due to intersections, changing speed limits, one way and multi-lane traffic. We considered maximum time period in both scenarios for our work. The time durations for the evaluation, in Table 1, are different for urban and highway because in the city, the vehicles have average of 1 to 3 h trip but the highway may have longer trips ranging from 3 to 6 h. Therefore, the highway scenario is evaluated for relatively longer duration that is 6 h.

6.1 Tracking Success Rate

Definition 1. *Tracking Success Rate (TSR) is the percentage of the successfully tracked vehicles which are at least once come in the contact of one of the listening stations.*

An unsuccessful event is considered when the eavesdropper does not accurately correlate the previous and new pseudonym and consider the new pseudonym to be associated with new vehicle. For the attacker, this brings the illusion of tracing a new vehicle and when such events occur in our experiments, the attacker is considered as unsuccessful in tracking, therefore, the overall TSR decreases when a large number of such events occur.

In Table 2, the highest TSR is observed for the periodical scheme in the highway scenario. This is due to longer eavesdropping on the unidirectional traffic. The continuous location updates and known pseudonym change interval of the vehicles ease the correlation of the new and old pseudonym for the attacker. Also, repetition of the pseudonyms introduces the higher tracking success rate as the vehicle can be tracked once the attacker has the knowledge of all twenty pseudonyms which can be obtained with sufficiently longer eavesdropping. In the urban traffic scenario, the tracking success rate is lower than highways but overall the attacker can track more than 80% of tracking success. SLOW scheme has shown better privacy protection against strategically placed local passive adversary. However, SLOW scheme outperforms periodical scheme in highway scenario and provide weak privacy protection with fifty percent of tracking success. Placement of the attacking station on the busy intersections increases the tracking success rate when using this scheme. Cooperative scheme is better than periodical and SLOW schemes because it has more randomized time which is not predictable. Therefore, placing the local passive listening stations in dense traffic areas such as city centers or nearby shopping malls increase the tracking rate. On the highways, the spatio-temporal information allows to correlate the old and new pseudonyms as the vehicles are moving at certain speed. On the other hand, CAPS scheme prevent the tracking relatively more than the other schemes. Especially in urban scenario, the TSR is 38.46 with the placement of the eavesdropping stations in the dense traffic areas as well as on the most used roads in the city.

Table 1. TSR and pseudonym usage in urban and highway scenario

PCS	Scenario	Traceability	Pseudonym usage
Periodical	Highway	97.22	70
	Urban	83.34	30
SLOW	Highway	50.26	95
	Urban	79.36	300
Cooperative	Highway	70.14	611
	Urban	42.43	129
CAPS	Highway	59.67	74
	Urban	38.46	25

6.2 Pseudonym Usage

The pseudonym usage is the important aspect of the pseudonym lifecycle. There is a set of limited number of these temporary identifiers which is given to the vehicle for duration of approximately three years [4]. Therefore, it is essential to use these pseudonyms efficiently without exhausting them in short time. PCS needs a trade-off between the pseudonym usage and the privacy protection. In our experiment, Table 2, we analyzed the level of privacy provided by different PCS with respect to the number of pseudonyms used. The pseudonym changing scheme which uses less number of pseudonyms is considered to be better. The periodical scheme has limited numbers of pseudonyms used over the time, this is because the scheme is solely based on the restrictive use of pseudonyms. However, the fixed interval of the change of pseudonym, elevate TSR due to repetition. For SLOW scheme, the number is higher in urban scenario. As the vehicle in city frequently slows down, therefore, every time the vehicle slows down near intersection due to red light or stop sign, it changes the pseudonym. The frequent changes force to use more number of the pseudonyms in small duration in urban scenario. While on highways, usually, the vehicles do not slow down up to speed of 30Km/hr, so we changed the speed trigger to 75 km/h which is possible as the slowing down speed on the highways. SLOW scheme is effective only if the frequency of pseudonym change does not matter. Cooperative scheme prevents the attack to some extent but at the cost of relatively very large number of pseudonyms. CAPS has uses pseudonyms comparable to periodical scheme but have the least TSR in both scenarios. Especially, in the urban scenarios, this scheme is more effective than others.

Table 2. TSR with varying number of eavesdropping stations

Stations	Vehicles	Periodical	SLOW	Cooperative	CAPS
2	30	43.4%	46.7%	24%	20.1%
3	56	46%	47.9%	29.3%	22.5%
4	76	78.9%	79.4%	51.3%	42.3%
6	84	89.3%	89.45%	64.54%	53.3%

6.3 Number of Eavesdropping Stations

The different number of attacking stations has impact on overall traceability of each PCS, as shown in Table 2. Ideally, the attacker would be interested in the urban areas where the number of vehicle is higher within relatively smaller area coverage. Therefore, we have taken into account the area of $3000\,m^2$ in urban city center. For the simulation, we generated 100 random trips for vehicles which enter and leaves the vehicular network within 300 s. Apparently, the vehicle leaves the network when it reaches the destination so some trips are shorter than the others. The area covered by each eavesdropping station is 300 m range. The Vehicle in the Table 2, refers to the total number of eavesdropped vehicles. As the number of eavesdropping stations increase (2, 3, 4, 6), TSR increases for all the schemes, however, the context-aware scheme provides reasonable protection against privacy attacks with 6 eavesdropping stations. It is important to note that the total observation area in the simulation scenario is small, therefore, having 6 eavesdropping stations results in significantly high TSR. Also, we mentioned the number of eavesdropped vehicles which is the subset of the total number of active vehicles in the scenario. Periodical and SLOW have increasing traceability rate with increasing number of stations, on the other hand, cooperative and context-aware have relatively less traceability. It is due to the reason that cooperative and context-aware schemes are dependent on the neighboring vehicles for pseudonym change and not all the vehicles would have neighbors for pseudonym change while moving nearby the eavesdropping stations.

7 Conclusion

To sum up our findings, in urban and highway scenarios, the local passive attacker is modeled to examine the effectiveness of the existing pseudonym changing schemes. These schemes are different from each other, however, our simulation observations considered a consistent privacy metric, TSR, for analysis and comparison of these schemes. The results show the least privacy protection for the schemes eases the prediction of the change in pseudonyms. We found that the dynamic and user centric schemes with the least number of pseudonyms usage are the most realistic and feasible among all the schemes. We also demonstrate the optimal case for an attacker to deploy the network of eavesdropping stations with the feasible attacking capabilities. Increase in the number of eavesdropping stations directly increase the tracking capabilities of the passive attacker.

For future work, we will investigate the effectiveness of pseudonym changing schemes against the other feasible attacking scenario with different attacking capabilities instead of the optimal case scenario. Also, we considered the same traffic for comparing the changing number of eavesdropper, in future, we intend to compare dense and sparse networks for the same.

References

1. Golle, P., Partridge, K.: On the anonymity of home/work location Pairs. In: Tokuda, H., Beigl, M., Friday, A., Brush, A.J.B., Tobe, Y. (eds.) Pervasive 2009. LNCS, vol. 5538, pp. 390–397. Springer, Heidelberg (2009). https://doi.org/10.1007/978-3-642-01516-8_26
2. Petit, J., et al.: Pseudonym schemes in vehicular networks: a survey. IEEE Commun. Surv. Tutor. **17**(1), 228–255 (2015)
3. https://www.its.dot.gov/resources/scms.htm
4. Brecht, B., et al.: A security credential management system for V2X communications. IEEE Trans. Intell. Transp. Syst. **99**, 1–22 (2018)
5. Pan, Y., Li, J.: Cooperative pseudonym change scheme based on the number of neighbors in vanets. J. Netw. Comput. Appl. **36**(6), 1599–1609 (2013)
6. Buttyan, L., Holczer, T., Weimerskirch, A., Whyte, W.: SLOW: a practical pseudonym changing scheme for location privacy in vanets. In: 2009 IEEE Vehicular Networking Conference (VNC), pp. 1–8. IEEE (2009)
7. Wasef, A., Shen, X.S.: REP: location privacy for vanets using random encryption periods. Mob. Netw. Appl. **15**(1), 172–185 (2010)
8. Freudiger, J., Raya, M., Félegyházi, M., Papadimitratos, P., Hubaux, J.-P.: Mixzones for location privacy in vehicular networks. In: ACM Workshop on Wireless Networking for Intelligent Transportation Systems (WiNITS), no. LCA-CONF-2007-016 (2007)
9. Eckhoff, D., Sommer, C., Gansen, T., German, R., Dressler, F.: Strong and affordable location privacy in VANETs: identity diffusion using time-slots and swapping. In: 2010 IEEE Vehicular Networking Conference (VNC), pp. 174–181. IEEE (2010)
10. Boualouache, A., Moussaoui, S.: S2SI: a practical pseudonym changing strategy for location privacy in VANETs. In: 2014 International Conference on Advanced Networking Distributed Systems and Applications (INDS), pp. 70–75. IEEE (2014)
11. Troncoso, C., Costa-Montenegro, E., Diaz, C., Schiffner, S.: On the difficulty of achieving anonymity for Vehicle-2-X communication. Comput. Netw. **55**(14), 3199–3210 (2011)
12. Wiedersheim, B., Ma, Z., Kargl, F., Papadimitratos, P.: Privacy in inter-vehicular networks: why simple pseudonym change is not enough. In: Proceedings of IEEE 7th International Conference on Wireless on Demand Network Systems and Services, pp. 176–183, February 2010

13. Emara, K., Wolfgang W., Schlichter, J.: CAPS: context-aware privacy scheme for VANET safety applications. In: Proceedings of the 8th ACM Conference on Security & Privacy in Wireless and Mobile Networks. ACM (2015)
14. Emara, K.: Poster: PREXT: privacy extension for veins VANET simulator. In: 2016 IEEE Vehicular Networking Conference (VNC). IEEE (2016)
15. Krajzewicz, D., et al.: Recent development and applications of SUMO-Simulation of Urban MObility. Int. J. Adv. Syst. Measur. 5 (2012)
16. Varga, A., Hornig, R.: An overview of the OMNeT++ simulation environment. In: Proceedings of the 1st International Conference on Simulation Tools and Techniques for Ccommunications, Networks and Systems and Workshops. ICST (Institute for Computer Sciences, Social-Informatics and Telecommunications Engineering) (2008)
17. Sommer, C., German, R., Dressler, F.: Bidirectionally coupled network and road traffic simulation for improved IVC analysis. IEEE Trans. Mob. Comput. 10(1), 3–15 (2011)
18. OpenStreetMap. https://www.openstreetmap.org/copyright. Accessed 08 Mar 2018

An RSA-Based User Authentication Scheme for Smart-Homes Using Smart Card

Maninder Singh Raniyal[1], Isaac Woungang[1(✉)],
and Sanjay Kumar Dhurandher[2]

[1] Department of Computer Science, Ryerson University, Toronto, ON, Canada
mraniyal@ryerson.ca, iwoungan@scs.ryerson.ca
[2] Division of Information Technology, NSIT, University of Delhi,
New Delhi, India
dhurandher@gmail.com

Abstract. Internet of Things (IoT) is an emerging paradigm which enables physical objects to operate over the Internet, collect and share the data that describe the real physical world. One of its greatest opportunity and application still lies ahead in the form of smart home, known as push-button automated home. In this ubiquitous environment, due to the most likely heterogeneity of objects, communication, topology, security protocols, and the computationally limited nature of IoT objects, conventional authentication schemes may not comply with IoT security requirements since they are considered impractical, weak, or outdated. Focusing only on the issue of remote authentication in a smart home environment, in the presence of security threats, this paper proposes the design of a RSA-based two-factor user Authentication scheme for Smart-Home using Smart Card (denoted RSA-ASH-SC scheme). An informal security analysis of the proposed RSA-ASH-SC scheme is proposed as well as a study of its performance in terms of convergence speed, showing that the RSA-ASH-SC scheme is about 50% faster than the Om and Kumari scheme, and about 15 times faster than selected RSA variants in terms of RSA decryption speed when the RSA key length is 2048. The RSA-ASH-SC scheme is also shown to maintain the anonymity of the user using a one-time token.

1 Introduction

Internet of Things (IoT) [1] has emerged as a driver for many applications in the area of smart homes, smart cities, to name a few. In IoT, devices (often referred to as objects) are often grouped into clusters, therefore, in order to enable secure communications across them, it is required that these objects be able to first authenticate with each other using cloud platforms or IoT-based communication protocols. However, most of these protocols do not possess inbuilt security mechanisms or rely on limited inbuilt single-factor authentication security mechanisms [2]. Focusing on a particular class of authentication methods for IoT devices in the cloud, namely one-time password (OTP), it has been reported [3] that most existing OTP schemes are not applicable in the smart home context because their designs would have to be substantially adjusted to fulfill the IoT requirements, in particular smart home requirements.

© Springer Nature Switzerland AG 2018
I. Traore et al. (Eds.): ISDDC 2018, LNCS 11317, pp. 16–29, 2018.
https://doi.org/10.1007/978-3-030-03712-3_2

In a smart home environment (Fig. 1), physical objects such as doors, temperature, alarms, alerts, appliances, to name a few, are equipped with the ability to operate over the Internet, for monitoring, collecting and sharing their resources (in particular their data) [2]. These objects are usually connected to each other through a Home Gateway (HG), an interface between the home network and the Internet. In order to control the smart home system, the HG has a routing functionality and is usually connected to the user interface using a mobile software, a well-mounted solution, to name a few.

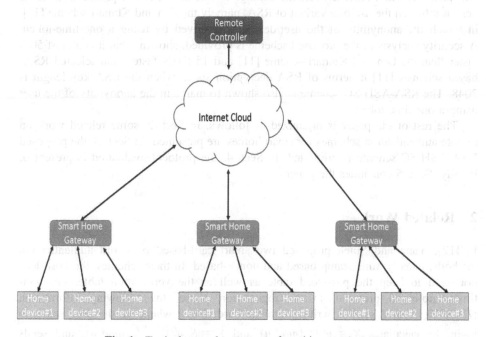

Fig. 1. Typical smart home network architecture in IoT.

In such an environment, there are essentially two types of authentication schemes: user authentication and device-to-device (D2D) authentication. In user-authentication schemes, some type of secrecy (known only by the user) or a unique biometric information of the user, is utilized for authentication purpose [4]. In the other hand, D2D authentication is also challenging since devices are usually heterogeneous, thus, are expected to operate under various different protocols and resource constraints such as energy restriction and security ones. In addition, communication technologies include radio waves and common radio wave technologies such as Ethernet 6LoW-PAN, Bluetooth LE (BLE), ZigBee, Z-Wave, to name a few. In the prospect of designing authentication protocols for a smart home networks, some minimal security requirements should also be met, namely: confidentiality, availability, integrity, and mutual authentication.

Considering the same smart home network architecture in IoT (Fig. 1), as far as user remote authentication for smart home environments is concerned, our literature survey has revealed that techniques based on passwords [5] are typically weak and are not considered very secure. To improve this weakness, other techniques have been proposed such as those relying on the user's personal memory or the use of Kerberos authentication to implement a single-sign-on [6], those relying on mobile OTP [7], an open standard authentication and authorization protocol in which the user receives a password that must be used within a short time period after its generation; those relying on smart cards [8], those relying on biometrics [9], those involving transactions based on Near Field Communications (NFC) [10]; those relying on RSA [11], to name a few. Our proposed RSA-ASH-SC scheme belongs to this later class of protocols since its design relies on the use of a variant of RSA, namely the Om and Kumari scheme [11], in which the anonymity of the user/device is achieved by using a one-time-token. A security analysis of the proposed scheme is provided, showing that it is almost 50% faster than the Om and Kumari scheme [11] and 15 times faster than selected RSA-based schemes [11] in terms of RSA decryption speed when the RSA key length is 2048. The RSA-ASH-SC scheme is also shown to maintain the anonymity of the user using a one-time token.

The rest of the paper is organized as follows. In Sect. 2, some related work on remote authentication schemes for smart homes are presented. In Sect. 3, the proposed RSA-ASH-SC scheme is presented. In Sect. 4, the protocol evaluation is presented. Finally, Sect. 5 concludes the paper.

2 Related Work

In [12], Yang and Shieh proposed two smart card-based password authentication methods, namely, time-stamp based and nonce-based. In their schemes, the host does not need to keep the password table as well as the verification table. For their timestamp-based protocol, in the registration phase, the following information $(ID_i, CID_i, h_i, S_i, e, g, n)$ is written into the card. Next, whenever the user wants to login, he calculates $X_i \equiv g^{r_i \cdot pw_i}(mod\ n)$ and $Y_i \equiv S_i.h_i^{r_i \cdot f(CID_i.T)}(mod\ n)$, and sends $(ID_i, CID_i, X_i, Y_i, e, g, n, T)$ to the host, which in turn verifies the following information: ID_i, CID_i and timestamp, then calculates $Y_i^e = ID_i.X_i^{f(CID_i.T)}$. If the equation holds true, the user gets authenticated. Chan and Cheng [13] and Sun and Yeh [14] performed a cryptanalysis of this scheme and reported that it is vulnerable to forgery attacks.

In [15], Fan et al. also performed a cryptanalysis of the Yang and Shieh scheme [12] and showed that it is vulnerable to impersonation attack. Based on their findings, they proposed an enhanced scheme which can be forged only with a valid CID_i, by imposing a restriction on ID_i so that an attacker cannot freely generate the ID_i.

In [5], Yang et al. also proposed an improvement of the timestamp-based authentication scheme proposed in [12]. In that scheme, the registration phase is not modified, but in the login phase, the user calculates $X_i = g^{pw_i \cdot r_i}(mod\ n)$ and $Y_i = S_i.h_i^{r_i \cdot T}(mod\ n)$, and sends $(ID_i, CID_i, X_i, Y_i, e, g, n, T)$ to the host. In the authentication phase, the host verifies the following information: ID_i, CID_i and timestamp and calculates $Y_i^e = ID_i^{CID_i}.X_i^T mod\ n$. If the equation holds true, the user gets authenticated.

They also performed a security analysis of this scheme, and verified that it is protected against forgery attack, password-guessing attack, smart-card loss attack and replay attack.

In [16], Shen et al. proposed a modified version of the Yang and Shieh scheme [12] scheme, transforming it to a mutual authentication scheme. They performed an analysis of the scheme in [12] and discovered that no relationship has been established between ID_i and CID_i, and without this, an intruder could bypass the remote server verification. In the modified scheme, a relationship between ID_i and CID_i at the registration phase is established a as follows: $CID_i = f(ID_i \oplus d)$, so that when the server receives the login request, it checks the validity of ID_i. Then, it calculates $CID_i' = f(ID_i \oplus d)$, and if CID_i' is equal to CID_i, the user gets authenticated.

In [17], Liu et al. proposed a remote user mutual authentication scheme for smart home as a result of a cryptanalysis of the Shen et al. scheme [45]. In their analysis, it was reported that if ID_i is chosen by a legitimate user, an attacker may be able to impersonate that user. In the modified Shen et al. scheme [16], to address this deficiency, instead of sending the CID_i, the user sends $f(CID_i)$ to the server, and a random nonce is used to challenge the user for mutual authentication purpose.

In [18], Chien et al. also proposed a remote user mutual authentication scheme for smart home, for which the security is based on the use of one-way hash functions. In their scheme, the server maintains a secret value x, and a timestamp is generated and attached to all messages that are exchanged between the user and the server, in order to protect against replay attack. However, a cryptanalysis of this scheme by Hsu [19] showed that it is vulnerable to parallel session attacks.

In [8], Om and Reddy proposed an RSA-based remote user authentication scheme using smart card. In their scheme, to achieve authentication, no verification table, nor password table is needed. Their scheme uses the standard RSA algorithm for cryptography as follows. In the registration phase, the user U_i submits its ID_i to the system, which in turn calculates $PW_i = ID_i^d \, mod \, \phi(n)$. It should be noted that a password generated in this way is difficult to remember for a user. Next, the smart card is issued with (f, ID_i, e, n). To login, the user calculates $x = PW_i \oplus T$, $y = ID_i^x (mod \, n)$ and $C = y^e (mod \, n)$. Then, sends the following message $S = (x, ID_i, C, T)$ to the server. Upon receipt, the server validates ID_i and the timestamp, then checks if $C^d (mod \, n) = y$. If that equation holds, the user gets authenticated. A cryptanalysis of this scheme by Om and Kumari [11] reveal that it is does not work properly for any given password.

In [11], Om and Kumari proposed a modified version of the Om and Reddy scheme [8] as follows. The registration phase is similar to that of the Om and Reddy scheme [8], except that additionally, the user calculates $S_i = f(PW_i \| ID_i)$ and stores it in the smart card. To login, the user calculates $x = f(f(PW_i \| ID_i) \oplus T) mod \, n$, $y = ID_i^x (mod \, n)$ and $C = y^e (mod \, n)$, then sends (ID_i, C, T) to the server. Upon receipt, the server checks for ID_i and the timestamp, then calculates $x = f(S_i \oplus T) mod \, n$, $y = ID_i^x mod \, n$ and $M = C^d mod \, n$. If $M = y$, the server authenticates the user. It should be noted that S_i is a sensitive information which is related to the password $S_i = f(PW_i \| ID_i)$; and S_i is also calculated when the user enters the password. If the smart card is lost, this information may lead to a compromised security [20]. Om and Kumari [11] also proposed a user remote authentication scheme based on the RPrime algorithm, a variant of RSA which is considered fast than the standard RSA [21]. In this scheme, at the registration time, the user chooses ID_i, PW_i and a random number N_i, then sends $\{ID_i, f(PW_i \oplus N_i)\}$ to the server. Next, the server calculates, $CID_i = f(ID_i \oplus d) mod \; \phi(n)$, $S_i = (CID_i \oplus f(PW_i \oplus N_i))^e mod \; n$ and $R_i = f(S_i\|N_i)$, where S_i is the sensitive information referred to in the Om and Reddy scheme [20], then stores the data (CID_i, R_i, n) in the smart card. This scheme was shown to be vulnerable to smart-card loss attack.

Unlike the above discussed schemes, our proposed scheme relies on a variant of RSA [11], in which the following additional features are introduced: the messages are kept encrypted, the anonymity of the device or user is achieved using a one-time-token, and a session key is established for any new session, and a timestamp is imposed on each message exchange between the user and the server in order to protect against replay attacks.

3 Proposed RSA-ASH-SC Scheme

We have considered the notations given in Table 1.

Table 1. Notations used in the proposed scheme

Notation	Description
$\phi(N)$	Euler's totient
n	Input security parameter for key generation algorithm
k	Distinct prime numbers in RSA key generation
s	Size of prime numbers in RSA key generation (Rebalanced)
p, q	Prime numbers used in RSA key generation
e	Encryption exponent
d	Decryption exponent
$mod()$	Modulus operation
$gcd()$	Greatest common divisor
$\oplus$	XOR operation
$h(), f()$	One way Hash function
ΔT	Threshold time used to prevent replay attack
$\{\}_{Si}$	Symmetric key encryption/decryption. Here Si is symmetric key
U_i	i^{th} user
ID_i	i^{th} user's ID
PW_i	i^{th} user's password
OTT_i	i^{th} user's One-Time-Token

The proposed RSA-ASH-SC scheme is a two-factor remote authentication scheme, the first of which is password (i.e. what you know factor) and the second is smart card (i.e. what you have factor). The user is required to register (one-time process) beforehand with the system. Each user U_i securely submits a hash of his chosen password PW_i and a smart card issuer generates a unique ID_i and other information, which are saved in the smart-card, to be used for remote user authentication purpose. Its steps are as follows:

Initialization Phase: The RSA keys are generated as per the method described in [23]. In our proposed scheme, the card issuer (in smart-home, the issuer can be himself) is the same as the authentication server/system. The key generation algorithm takes two security parameters as inputs: n and k. First, it generates n/k bits long two prime numbers p and q, such that $gcd((p-1),(q-1)) = 2$. Then, it calculates $N = p^{(k-1)}.q$. Next, it generates two random numbers $r1$ and $r2$ in such a way that $gcd(r1,(p-1)) = 1$, $gcd(r2,(q-1)) = 1$ and $r1 = r2 \ mod(2)$. Then, it finds the integer d such that $d = r1 \ mod(p-1)$ and $d = r2 \ mod(q-1)$. Finally, it calculates e such that $e = d^{-1}mod(\phi(N))$. Here, the public key is (e, N) and the private key is $(p, q, r1, r2)$, which is kept secret with the card issuer.

Registration Phase: The user submits a request, in secure manner, to the issuer for the smart card by sharing the hash of his password $HPW_i = h(PW_i)$, where $h()$ is a one-way hash function and PW_i is the password of the user. Upon receiving the request, the issuer-server creates a random and unique ID_i for the user. The server also creates a random one-time-token OTT_i to keep the future authentication requests. Next, the server calculates $HPWID_i = h(HPW_i \oplus ID_i)$ and stores this value and OTT_i in its database, which is protected by its private key. Next, the server stores the following information (ID_i, OTT_i, h, e, N) on the smart card. The smart card is then physically handled over to the user.

Login Phase: The user requires a smart card reader before starting the login process. First, the user connects the smart card reader and writer (SCRW) to the personal digital assistant (PDA). Then, he opens the application which makes use of the proposed authentication. The user enters the password PW_i which is sent to the card, for example, using an application protocol data unit (APDU) [24]. This application also generates and sends a random secret key S_i to the smart card. It should be noted that the secret key is generated for every new session. The card then performs the following steps. First, it computes x as $x = (h((h(PW_i) \oplus ID_i))^e \oplus h(T))mod \ N$, where T is a newly created timestamp. Then, it computes $HXOTT_i = h(x \oplus OTT_i$. Next, it computes $y = (OTT_i \parallel T \parallel S_i \parallel h(OTT_i \parallel T \parallel S_i \parallel HXOTT_i) \parallel HXOTT_i)$ and encrypts y as $C = y^e mod(N)$, then sends the following message (OTT_i, C) to the server.

Authentication Phase: Upon receipt, the server compares OTT_i against the entries in the database. If there is a match, it decrypts the message. To achieve this, it computes $M_1 = C^{r1}mod(p)$ and $M_2 = C^{r2}mod(q)$. Using CRT, it calculates $M \in Z_N$ such that $M = M_1 mod(p)$ and $M = M_2 mod(q)$. The received message $M = (OTT_i \parallel T \parallel S_i \parallel h(OTT_i \parallel T \parallel S_i \parallel HXOTT_i) \parallel HXOTT_i)$. Then, it checks whether the timestamp is recent or not, i.e. $(T_c - T) < \Delta T$, where T_c is the current time and ΔT is the acceptable timestamp difference. It also verifies OTT_i within message M again with the unencrypted OTT_i. It also verifies the hash of the message to check if the message was tempered. Then, it computes $x = ((HPWID_i)^e \oplus h(T))mod \ N$ and $Z = h(x \oplus OTT_i)$. If Z and $HXOTT_i$ are equal, it authenticates the request. The server then creates a new random token OTT_{new} and current timestamp T_{new}, then computes the response as $M_r = (T_{new}, \{h(T_{new} \parallel OTT_{new}), OTT_{new}\}_{S_i})$ and sends that response to the user. Here, $\{\}_{S_i}$ is the encryption/decryption function and S_i is the symmetric key. The server also updates the token (OTT_i) of the corresponding ID_i with OTT_{new}. When the user receives the response, it decrypts the message $M = (T_{new}, \{\{h(T_{new} \parallel OTT_{new}), OTT_{new}\}_{S_i}\}_{Si})$. First, it checks whether the timestamp is recent or not, i.e. $(T_c - T_{new}) < \Delta T$. If it is the case, it stores the new token OTT_{new} in the card for the new time and uses S_i for further communication; otherwise it drops the authentication request.

Password Change: To update the password, the user needs to be authenticated in advance. The user enters its password and calculates the hash of the new password as $HPW_{new} = h(PW_{new})$, then sends a password update command to the server as $CMD = \{pass_{update}, T, h(T, HPW_{new}), HPW_{new}\}_{Si}$, where $pass_{update}$ is a known command to the server. After receiving the command, the server decrypts the message using S_i and validates the timestamp and hash of the message as described above. If validated, the server computes $HPWID_{new} = h(HPW_{new} \oplus ID_i)$, then updates the $HPWID_i$ in the database corresponding to the user ID_i.

The proposed RSA-ASH-SC Scheme can be summarized as follows:

Client <-->   **Server**
$x = (h((h(PW_i) \oplus ID_i))^e \oplus h(T)) \bmod N$
$HXOTT_i = h(x \oplus OTT_i)$
$y = (OTT_i \parallel T \parallel S_i \parallel h(OTT_i \parallel T \parallel S_i \parallel HXOTT_i) \parallel HXOTT_i)$
$C = y^e \bmod (N)$
$$(OTT_i, C)$$
$\xrightarrow{\hspace{7cm}}$

$M_1 = C^{r1} \bmod (p)$
$\qquad M_2 = C^{r2} \bmod (q)$
Using CRT $M \in Z_N$
$\quad M = (OTT_i \parallel T \parallel S_i \parallel h(OTT_i \parallel T \parallel S_i \parallel HXOTT_i) \parallel HXOTT_i)$
If $(T_c - T) < \Delta T$
Verify OTT_i
$x = ((HPWID_i)^e \oplus h(T)) \bmod N$
$Z = h(x \oplus OTT_i)$
If $Z == HXOTT_i$
Create OTT_{new} and T_{new}
$\quad M_r = (T_{new}, \{h(T_{new} \parallel OTT_{new}), OTT_{new}\}_{Si})$
$$(M_r)$$
$\qquad\qquad M = (T_{new}, \{\{h(T_{new} \parallel OTT_{new}), OTT_{new}\}_{Si}\}_{Si})$
$\xleftarrow{\hspace{7cm}}$

If $(T_c - T_{new}) < \Delta T$
Updates OTT_{new}

4   Informal Security Analysis

First, an informal security analysis of our proposed RSA-ASH-SC scheme is presented as follows.

Forgery Attack: In our scheme, the anonymity is ensured by the use of one-time tokens. The attacker cannot get any information from the one-time token and encrypted message. The encryption and decryption operations are performed by using Rebalanced-Multi-Power RSA variant [8]. The login message makes use of a password, a unique ID which is associated with a user and a timestamp. For attacker, there is no way to gain this information as the communication is encrypted.

Replay Attack: In our scheme, a timestamp is utilized to calculate $x = (h((h(PW_i) \oplus ID_i))^e \oplus h(T)) mod\ N$, which is used to construct the login message, which in turn will be different each time. Therefore, the adversary cannot launch a replay attack.

Man-in-the-Middle Attack (MIMA): In our scheme, since our messages are encrypted and only OTT_i is given in plaintext which is only for one-time use. The attacker cannot perform this type of attack, unless he knows PW_i, ID_i and OTT_i in advance.

Password-Guessing Attack: In our scheme, to guess the password, the adversary needs to decrypt the login message, which is infeasible it is protected by the private key. The other way that the adversary could try is to compromise the server and get its password database; but this is not an easy task since the database itself is protected by the private key, thus, this type of attack cannot be launch by an attacker.

Smart-Card Loss Attack: In case, the smart-card is lost or stolen, the adversary can try to get ID_i and OTT_i from the smart-card using invasive attacks [20], which is difficult. However, the adversary cannot get the password information. Therefore, he cannot compromise the security.

Denial of Service (DoS) Attack: The server only requires to check OTT_i to decide if a valid user is trying to authenticate. If OTT_i is not valid, the server can discard the login request without processing the encrypted message, which in turn requires very less computation compared to if it has to perform the hash of symmetric/asymmetric decryption. Even if the attacker makes use of a valid OTT_i by eavesdropping, the server will be able to identify the particular OTT_i used for DoS attack and report the incident to the administrator. The administrator can then set firewall rules to drop the login requests which make use of that OTT_i; this operation may temporarily disable the user associated with OTT_i, but the administrator can ask the user to manually update OTT_i over the secure channel.

Second, the proposed RSA-ASH-SC scheme is qualitatively compared against some selected RSA-based variants in terms of few security attacks (as per Table 2).

Third, the proposed RSA-ASH-SC scheme is quantitatively compared against the selected RSA-based variants (listed in Table 4) in terms of computational performance. Our findings are captured in Table 3, where T_{exp} is the time taken by modular exponent operation, T_{mul} is the time taken by the modular multiplication operation, T_h is the time taken by hash function operation, T_{xor} is the time taken by the XOR operation, T_e is the time taken by the modular encryption exponent *(e)* operation, T_d is the time taken by the modular decryption exponent *(d)* operation, and T_s is the time taken to encrypt and decrypt using the symmetric key.

Table 2. Comparison of selected RSA variants w.r.t. to security attacks and few security metrics.

	Yang et al. [12]	Fan et al. [15]	Yang et al. [5]	Om et al. [8]	Om et al. [21]	Shen et al. [16]	Liu et al. [17]	Chien et al. [18]	Proposed RSA-ASH-SC scheme
Confidentiality	✓	✓	✓	✓	✓	✓	✓	✓	✓
Availability	✓	✓						✓	✓
Integrity						✓		✓	✓
Mutual authentication						✓	✓	✓	✓
MIMA				✓	✓	✓	✓		✓
Stolen-card loss attack	✓	✓	✓			✓	✓	✓	✓
Password-guessing attack	✓	✓	✓	✓	✓	✓	✓	✓	✓
Replay attack	✓	✓	✓	✓	✓	✓	✓		✓
Forgery or impersonation			✓	✓	✓		✓		✓
DoS attack	✓	✓						✓	✓
Forward secrecy	✓	✓				✓	✓		

Based on Table 3, it is found that Chien et al. [18] scheme yields less computation time compared to other schemes.

Table 3. Comparison of selected RSA variants w.r.t. to computation performance

	Login phase	Authentication phase
Yang et al. [12]	$2T_{exp} + 3T_{mul} + T_h$	$T_e + T_{exp} + T_{mul} + T_h$
Fan et al. [15]	$2T_{exp} + 3T_{mul} + T_h$	$T_e + T_{exp} + T_{mul} + T_h$
Yang et al. [5]	$2T_{exp} + 3T_{mul}$	$T_e + 2T_{exp} + T_{mul}$
Om et al. [8]	$T_e + T_{exp} + T_h + T_{xor}$	T_d
Om et al. [11]	$T_e + T_{exp} + 2T_h + T_{xor}$	$T_d + T_{exp} + T_h + T_{xor}$
Shen et al. [16]	$T_e + 2T_{exp} + 3T_{mul} + 2T_h$	$T_d + 2T_h + T_{xor}$
Liu et al. [17]	$T_d + T_e + T_{exp} + T_{mul} + 2T_h + 2T_{xor}$	$T_e + 2T_h + T_{xor} + 3T_{mul} + 2T_{exp}$
Chien et al. [18]	$2T_h + 2T_{xor}$	$3T_h + 3T_{xor}$
Proposed RSA-ASH-SC scheme	$2T_e + T_s + 6T_h + 2T_{xor}$	$T_d + T_e + 2T_h + 2T_{xor} + T_s$

Fourth, the proposed RSA-ASH-SC scheme is a RSA-based protocol. As such, it performance in terms of speed of convergence is heavily dependent on that of the considered RSA underlying algorithm. Inspired from a study carried in [25], the impact of the performance of the RSA underlying algorithm (including selected RSA variants' performance) on the performance of the proposed RSA-ASH-SC scheme is quantified in terms of speed of convergence.

According to the Crypto++ benchmark [25], the RSA decryption is much slower in performance than the RSA encryption. Indeed, it was reported [10] that with a key length of 2048, the RSA encryption takes only 0.03 ms/operation to complete whereas the decryption algorithm takes 1.03 ms/operation, on the Fedora Operating system, Release 25 (x86_64), where the host CPU is a 6th generation Skylake, with a frequency *3.14e + 9 Hz*. Because of this, in the sequel, when we refer to *"decryption perfor- mance"*, we mean *"the performance of the RSA algorithm as a whole in terms of how fast it converges"*. This convention prevails for all RSA variants referred to in this Subsection, which have been proposed in the literature and validated as improvements to the decryption performance of the standard RSA algorithm [22], i.e. to speed up the decryption process, namely the Batch RSA scheme [26], the Multi-Prime RSA scheme [27], the Multi-Power RSA scheme [28], Rebalanced RSA scheme [29], the RPrime RSA scheme [21], and a combination of Rebalanced RSA and Multi-Power RSA scheme (here referred to as Rebalanced-Multi-Power RSA scheme [23]).

According to a performance study of these RSA variants using a 1024 bits key size [30], and considering the cost of a single modular exponentiation, the Batch RSA scheme [26] can compute several modular exponentiations effectively. In fact, it was reported that a batch size of 4 (resp. 8) increases the decryption performance of RSA by a factor of 2.6 (resp. 3.5).

For the Multi-Prime RSA scheme [27], which generates k distinct prime numbers (using the same key size of 1024), it was reported that k should be less or equal to 3 and the decryption process requires k full exponentiations modulo n/k bit numbers to complete. In contrast, running the standard RSA in conjunction with the Chinese Remainder Theorem [22], it was reported [30] that to calculate $xd\ mod\ p$, it takes $O(logd.\log^2 p)$, and if d is at the same scale of p, the decryption performance of Multi-Prime RSA scheme [27] is $\left(2.\left(\frac{n}{2}\right)^3\right)/k.\left(\frac{n}{k}\right)^3 = k^2/4$ better than that of the standard RSA [22].

For the Multi-Power RSA scheme [28], where the moduli is formed as $N = p^{k-1}.q$, where p and q are two distinct primes of n/k bits each, it was reported [30] that two full exponentiations modulo n/b bits are required for the completion of the decryption, yielding a decryption performance of $\left(2.\left(\frac{n}{2}\right)^3\right)/2.\left(\frac{n}{k}\right)^3 = k^3/8$ better than that of the standard RSA [22].

For the Rebalanced RSA scheme [29], where *two* prime numbers of $n/2$ bits size each are created and an input parameter $s \leq n/2$ is used to generate the decryption key, it was reported [30] that the decryption performance is $(n/2)/s = n/2s$ better than that of the original RSA [22].

For the RPrime scheme [21], which was designed as a combination of the Rebalanced RSA scheme [29] and the Multi-Prime RSA scheme [27], and in which

k distinct prime numbers using a key size of 1024 is generated as in Multi-Prime RSA scheme [27], it was reported [30] that the decryption performance is $k^2/4.n/ks = n.k/4.s$ better than that of the standard RSA [22].

For the Rebalanced-Multi-Power RSA scheme [23], which was designed as a combination of the Rebalanced RSA [29] and Multi-Power RSA scheme [28], it was reported [30] that the decryption performance is $k^3/8.n/ks = n.k^2/8.s$ better than that of the standard RSA [22].

Table 4 highlights the performance comparison of the above RSA variants [30] in terms of convergence speed. It can be observed an increase in k (the number of prime factors used in the RSA algorithm) also yields an increase in the decryption performance of the above discussed RSA variants.

Table 4. Decryption performance of selected RSA variants [30]

RSA variant	Decryption performance
Standard RSA [22]	x
Batch RSA [26]	$2.6\ x(if\ batch\_size = 4); 3.5\ x(if\ batch\_size = 8)$
Multi-Prime RSA [27]	$(k^2/4).x$
Multi-Power RSA [23]	$(k^3/8).x$
Rebalanced RSA [29]	$(n/2.s).x$
RPrime RSA [21]	$(n.k/4.s).x$
Rebalanced-Multi-Power RSA [23] (used in our RSA-ASH-SC scheme)	$(n.k^2/8.s).x$

In order to estimate the performance of our proposed RSA-ASH-SC scheme in terms of convergence speed, we have considered the Rebalanced-Multi-Power RSA scheme [23] as underlying RSA algorithm, using a key length of 1024 bits (as above), but also a key length of 2048 bits (as per the NIST recommendation [31]). Using the results shown in Table 4, the comparison of the RSA variants in term of decryption performance when k = 3 are captured in Fig. 2, where it can be observed that independently of the RSA key length, our proposed scheme is about 50% faster than the Om and Kumari scheme [11]. For a RSA key length of 2048 bits with k = 3, our proposed scheme is about 14.4% faster than any of the other considered RSA variants. For a RSA key length of 1024 bits with k = 3, our proposed scheme is about 7.2% faster than the Om and Kumari scheme [11], which itself is 9.6 time faster than the standard RSA for a key length 2048 (resp. 4.8 times faster for a RSA key length 1028) [23]. It is also observed that independently of the key length, our scheme outperforms the other studied schemes when k = 3. Hence, our proposed scheme yields a better decryption performance compared to the other studied schemes.

Lecture Notes in Computer Science 11251

Commenced Publication in 1973
Founding and Former Series Editors:
Gerhard Goos, Juris Hartmanis, and Jan van Leeuwen

Editorial Board

David Hutchison
Lancaster University, Lancaster, UK
Takeo Kanade
Carnegie Mellon University, Pittsburgh, PA, USA
Josef Kittler
University of Surrey, Guildford, UK
Jon M. Kleinberg
Cornell University, Ithaca, NY, USA
Friedemann Mattern
ETH Zurich, Zurich, Switzerland
John C. Mitchell
Stanford University, Stanford, CA, USA
Moni Naor
Weizmann Institute of Science, Rehovot, Israel
C. Pandu Rangan
Indian Institute of Technology Madras, Chennai, India
Bernhard Steffen
TU Dortmund University, Dortmund, Germany
Demetri Terzopoulos
University of California, Los Angeles, CA, USA
Doug Tygar
University of California, Berkeley, CA, USA
Gerhard Weikum
Max Planck Institute for Informatics, Saarbrücken, Germany

More information about this series at http://www.springer.com/series/7409

Tran Khanh Dang · Josef Küng
Roland Wagner · Nam Thoai
Makoto Takizawa (Eds.)

Future Data and Security Engineering

5th International Conference, FDSE 2018
Ho Chi Minh City, Vietnam, November 28–30, 2018
Proceedings

Editors
Tran Khanh Dang
Ho Chi Minh City University of Technology
Ho Chi Minh, Vietnam

Josef Küng
Johannes Kepler University of Linz
Linz, Austria

Roland Wagner
Johannes Kepler University of Linz
Linz, Austria

Nam Thoai
Ho Chi Minh City University of Technology
Ho Chi Minh, Vietnam

Makoto Takizawa
Hosei University
Tokyo, Japan

ISSN 0302-9743   ISSN 1611-3349   (electronic)
Lecture Notes in Computer Science
ISBN 978-3-030-03191-6   ISBN 978-3-030-03192-3   (eBook)
https://doi.org/10.1007/978-3-030-03192-3

Library of Congress Control Number: 2018959232

LNCS Sublibrary: SL3 – Information Systems and Applications, incl. Internet/Web, and HCI

This Springer imprint is published by the registered company Springer Nature Switzerland AG
The registered company address is: Gewerbestrasse 11, 6330 Cham, Switzerland

Preface

In this volume we present the accepted contributions for the 5th International Conference on Future Data and Security Engineering (FDSE 2018). The conference took place during November 28–30, 2018, in Ho Chi Minh City, Vietnam, at HCMC University of Technology, among the most famous and prestigious universities in Vietnam. The proceedings of FDSE are published in the LNCS series by Springer. Besides DBLP and other major indexing systems, FDSE proceedings have also been indexed by Scopus and listed in Conference Proceeding Citation Index (CPCI) of Thomson Reuters.

The annual FDSE conference is a premier forum designed for researchers, scientists, and practitioners interested in state-of-the-art and state-of-the-practice activities in data, information, knowledge, and security engineering to explore cutting-edge ideas, to present and exchange their research results and advanced data-intensive applications, as well as to discuss emerging issues in data, information, knowledge, and security engineering. At the annual FDSE, the researchers and practitioners are not only able to share research solutions to problems in today's data and security engineering themes, but also able to identify new issues and directions for future related research and development work.

The call for papers resulted in the submission of 122 papers. A rigorous and peer-review process was applied to all of them. This resulted in 35 accepted papers (including seven short papers, acceptance rate: 28.69%) and two keynote speeches, which were presented at the conference. Every paper was reviewed by at least three members of the international Program Committee, who were carefully chosen based on their knowledge and competence. This careful process resulted in the high quality of the contributions published in this volume. The accepted papers were grouped into the following sessions:

- Security and privacy engineering
- Authentication and access control
- Big data analytics and applications
- Advanced studies in machine learning
- Deep learning and applications
- Data analytics and recommendation systems
- Internet of Things and applications
- Smart city: data analytics and security
- Emerging data management systems and applications

In addition to the papers selected by the Program Committee, five internationally recognized scholars delivered keynote speeches: "Freely Combining Partial Knowledge in Multiple Dimensions," presented by Prof. Dirk Draheim from Tallinn University of Technology, Estonia; "Programming Data Analysis Workflows for the Masses," presented by Prof. Artur Andrzejak from Heidelberg University, Germany; "Mathematical

Foundations of Machine Learning: A Tutorial," presented by Prof. Dinh Nho Hao from Institute of Mathematics, Vietnam Academy of Science and Technology; "4th Industry Revolution Technologies and Security," presented by Prof. Tai M. Chung from Sungkyunkwan University, South Korea; and "Risk-Based Software Quality and Security Engineering in Data-Intensive Environments," presented by Prof. Michael Felderer from University of Innsbruck, Austria.

The success of FDSE 2018 was the result of the efforts of many people, to whom we would like to express our gratitude. First, we would like to thank all authors who submitted papers to FDSE 2018, especially the invited speakers for the keynotes and tutorials. We would also like to thank the members of the committees and external reviewers for their timely reviewing and lively participation in the subsequent discussion in order to select such high-quality papers published in this volume. Last but not least, we thank the Faculty of Computer Science and Engineering, HCMC University of Technology, for hosting and organizing FDSE 2018.

November 2018   Tran Khanh Dang
                                                       Josef Küng
                                                   Roland Wagner
                                                       Nam Thoai
                                                  Makoto Takizawa

Organization

General Chair

Roland Wagner   Johannes Kepler University Linz, Austria

Steering Committee

Elisa Bertino   Purdue University, USA
Dirk Draheim   Tallinn University of Technology, Estonia
Kazuhiko Hamamoto   Tokai University, Japan
Koichiro Ishibashi   The University of Electro-Communications, Japan
M-Tahar Kechadi   University College Dublin, Ireland
Dieter Kranzlmüller   Ludwig Maximilian University, Germany
Fabio Massacci   University of Trento, Italy
Clavel Manuel   The Madrid Institute for Advanced Studies in Software
                               Development Technologies, Spain
Atsuko Miyaji   Osaka University and Japan Advanced Institute
                               of Science and Technology, Japan
Erich Neuhold   University of Vienna, Austria
Cong Duc Pham   University of Pau, France
Silvio Ranise   Fondazione Bruno Kessler, Italy
Nam Thoai   HCMC University of Technology, Vietnam
A Min Tjoa   Technical University of Vienna, Austria
Xiaofang Zhou   The University of Queensland, Australia

Program Committee Chairs

Tran Khanh Dang   HCMC University of Technology, Vietnam
Josef Küng   Johannes Kepler University Linz, Austria
Makoto Takizawa   Hosei University, Japan

Publicity Chairs

Nam Ngo-Chan   University of Trento, Italy
Quoc Viet Hung Nguyen   The University of Queensland, Australia
Huynh Van Quoc Phuong   Johannes Kepler University Linz, Austria
Tran Minh Quang   HCMC University of Technology, Vietnam
Le Hong Trang   HCMC University of Technology, Vietnam

Local Organizing Committee

Tran Khanh Dang	HCMC University of Technology, Vietnam
Tran Tri Dang	HCMC University of Technology, Vietnam
Josef Küng	Johannes Kepler University Linz, Austria
Nguyen Dinh Thanh	Data Security Applied Research Lab, Vietnam
Que Nguyet Tran Thi	HCMC University of Technology, Vietnam
Tran Ngoc Thinh	HCMC University of Technology, Vietnam
Tuan Anh Truong	HCMC University of Technology, Vietnam and University of Trento, Italy
Quynh Chi Truong	HCMC University of Technology, Vietnam
Nguyen Thanh Tung	HCMC University of Technology, Vietnam

Finance and Leisure Chairs

Hue Anh La	HCMC University of Technology, Vietnam
Hoang Lan Le	HCMC University of Technology, Vietnam

Program Committee

Artur Andrzejak	Heidelberg University, Germany
Stephane Bressan	National University of Singapore, Singapore
Hyunseung Choo	Sungkyunkwan University, South Korea
Tai M. Chung	Sungkyunkwan University, South Korea
Agostino Cortesi	Università Ca' Foscari Venezia, Italy
Bruno Crispo	University of Trento, Italy
Nguyen Tuan Dang	University of Information Technology, VNUHCM, Vietnam
Agnieszka Dardzinska-Glebocka	Bialystok University of Technology, Poland
Tran Cao De	Can Tho University, Vietnam
Thanh-Nghi Do	Can Tho University, Vietnam
Nguyen Van Doan	Japan Advanced Institute of Science and Technology, Japan
Dirk Draheim	Tallinn University of Technology, Estonia
Nguyen Duc Dung	HCMC University of Technology, Vietnam
Johann Eder	Alpen-Adria University Klagenfurt, Austria
Jungho Eom	Daejeon University, South Korea
Verena Geist	Software Competence Center Hagenberg, Austria
Raju Halder	Indian Institute of Technology Patna, India
Tran Van Hoai	HCMC University of Technology, Vietnam
Nguyen Quoc Viet Hung	The University of Queensland, Australia
Nguyen Viet Hung	Bosch, Germany
Trung-Hieu Huynh	Industrial University of Ho Chi Minh City, Vietnam
Tomohiko Igasaki	Kumamoto University, Japan
Muhammad Ilyas	University of Sargodha, Pakistan

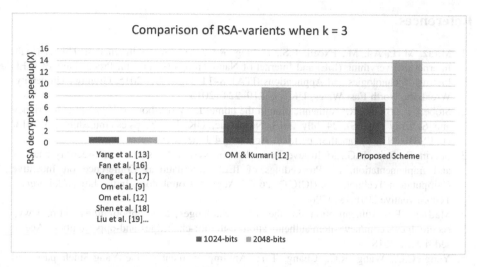

Fig. 2. Convergence speed of selected RSA variants for key length 1024 bits vs. 2048 bits when k = 3.

5 Conclusion

In this paper, we have proposed a novel RSA-based two-factor remoted user authentication scheme for smart-home using smart card (called RSA-ASH-SC scheme). An informal security analysis of the proposed RSA-ASH-SC scheme has been conducted; as well as its performance with respect to the convergence speed. For this performance study, we have considered the Rebalanced-Multi-Power RSA scheme [8] as underlying RSA algorithm of our RSA-ASH-SC scheme, using respectively a key length of 1024 bits and 2048 bits, the results have shown that: (1) Using a key length of 1028 (resp. 2048) with k = 3, where k is the number of prime factors used in the RSA scheme, our proposed RSA-ASH-SC scheme is about 50% faster than the Om and Kumari scheme; (2) Using a key length of 2048 bits with k = 3, our proposed RSA-ASH-SC scheme is about 15% faster than any of the other considered RSA variants; (3) Using a key length of 1024 bits with k = 3, our proposed RSA-ASH-SC scheme is about 7.2% faster than the Om and Kumari scheme. We have also compare some selected RSA variants with respect to few security attacks and selected security metrics. Except for the Forward Secrecy attack, which our RSA-ASH-SC scheme may not prevent, all other considered attacks could be prevented based on its design features.

As future work, in the proposed RSA-ASH-SC scheme, the session keys are created by a client, and then encrypted and sent to the server over a network. If the RSA keys are compromised, the scheme will become vulnerable to forwards secrecy attack. To protect against this attack, the session keys should be exchanged in a secure manner, for instance, using the Diffie-Hellman key exchange protocol. The proposed RSA-ASH-SC approach could also be re-designed to rely biometric rather than smart card. It can also be adjusted to rely on the three factors: smart card, password, and biometric. The tight coupling of these three factors will add more security layers; yielding a much stronger authentication mechanism for smart home networks.

References

1. Miraz, M.H., Ali, M., Excell, P.S., Picking, R.: A review on Internet of Things (IoT), Internet of Everything (IoE) and Internet of Nano Things (IoNT). In: Proceedings of IEEE Internet Technologies and Applications (ITA), 8–11 September 2015, Glyndwr University, Wrexham, North East Wales, UK, pp. 219–224 (2015)
2. Stobert, E., Biddle, R.: Authentication in the home. In: Workshop on Home Usable Privacy and Security (HUPS), 24 July 2013, Newcastle, UK. http://cups.cs.cmu.edu/soups/2013/HUPS/HUPS13-ElizabethStobert.pdf. Accessed 4 June 2018
3. Sherin, P., Raju, K.G.: Multi-level authentication system for smart home-security analysis and implementation. In: Proceedings of IEEE International Conference on Incentive Computation Technologies (ICICT), 26–27 August, Coimbatore, India. https://doi.org/10.1109/inventive.2016.7824790
4. Madsen, P.: Authentication in the IoT: challenges and opportunities. http://www.secureidnews.com/news-item/authentication-in-the-iot-challenges-and-opportunities. Accessed 4 June 2018
5. Yang, C.C., Wang, R.C., Chang, T.Y.: An improvement of the Yang-Shieh password authentication schemes. Appl. Math. Comput. **162**, 1391–1396 (2005)
6. Gaikwad, P.P., Gabhane, J.P., Golait, S.S.: 3-level secure kerberos authentication for smart home systems using IoT. In: Proceedings of 1st IEEE International Conference on Next Generation Computing Technologies (NGCT), 4–5 September 2015, Dehradun, India, pp. 262–268 (2015)
7. Borgohain, T., Borgohain, A., Kumar, U., Sanyal, S.: Authentication Systems in Internet of Things. https://arxiv.org/abs/1502.00870. Accessed 4 June 2018
8. Om, H., Reddy, M.: RSA based remote password authentication using smart card. J. Discrete Math. Sci. Cryptography **15**(2), 105–111 (2012)
9. Wang, X., Zhang, W.: An efficient and secure biometric remote user authentication scheme using smart cards. In: Proceedings of Pacific-Asia Workshop on Computational Intelligence and Industrial Application (PACIIA 2008), 19–20 December 2008, Wuhan, China, pp. 913–917 (2008). https://doi.org/10.1109/paciia.2008.382
10. Remote user authentication using NFC, US patent US20110212707. https://www.google.ch/patents/US20110212707. Accessed 4 June 2018
11. Om, H., Kumari, S.: Comment and modification of RSA based remote password authentication using smart card. J. Discrete Math. Sci. Cryptography 625–635 (2017)
12. Yang, W.H., Shieh, S.P.: Password authentication schemes with smart cards. Comput. Secur. **18**(8), 727–733 (1999)
13. Chan, C.K., Cheng, L.M.: Cryptanalysis of a timestamp-based password authentication scheme. Comput. Secur. **21**(I), 74–76 (2002)
14. Sun, H.M., Yeh, H.T.: Further cryptanalysis of a password authentication scheme with smart cards. IEICE Trans. Commun. **E86-B**(4), 1412–1415 (2003)
15. Fan, L., Li, J.H., Zhu, H.W.: An enhancement of timestamp based password authentication scheme. Comput. Secur. **21**, 665–667 (2002)
16. Shen, J.J., Lin, C.W., Hwang, M.S.: Security enhancement for the timestamp-based password authentication scheme using smart cards. Comput. Secur. **22**(7), 591–595 (2003)
17. Liu, Y., Zhou, A.M., Gao, M.X.: A new mutual authentication scheme based on nonce and smart cards. Comput. Commun. **31**(10), 2205–2209 (2008)
18. Chien, H.Y., Jan, J.K., Tseng, Y.M.: An efficient and practical solution to remote authentication: smart card. Comput. Secur. **21**(4), 372–375 (2002)

19. Hsu, C.L.: Security of Chien et al.'s remote user authentication scheme using smart cards. Comput. Stand. Interfaces (2003)
20. Bar-El, H.: Known Attacks Against Smart cards. http://www.infosecwriters.com/text_resources/pdf/Known_Attacks_Against_Smartcards.pdf. Accessed 4 June 2018
21. Paixao, C.A.M., Filho, D.L.G.: An efficient variant of the RSA cryptosystem. Eprint Archive (2003)
22. Rivest, R.L., Shamir, A., Adleman, L.: A method for obtaining digital signatures and public-key cryptosystems. Commun. ACM **21**(2), 120–126 (1978)
23. Garg, D., Verma, S.: Improvement over public key cryptographic algorithm. In: IEEE International Advance Computing Conference (IACC 2009), Patiala, India, March 2009
24. Smart card application protocol data unit. https://en.wikipedia.org/wiki/Smart_card_application_protocol_data_unit. Accessed 4 June 2018
25. Crypto++ Benchmark. https://www.cryptopp.com/benchmarks.html. Accessed 28 Nov 2017
26. Fiat, A.: Batch RSA. In: Brassard, G. (ed.) CRYPTO 1989. LNCS, vol. 435, pp. 175–185. Springer, New York (1990). https://doi.org/10.1007/0-387-34805-0_17
27. Collins, T., Hopkins, D., Langford, S., Sabin, M.: Public Key Cryptographic Apparatus and Method. US Patent #5848159, January 1997
28. Takagi, T.: Fast RSA-type cryptosystem modulo $p^k q$. In: Krawczyk, H. (ed.) CRYPTO 1998. LNCS, vol. 1462, pp. 318–326. Springer, Heidelberg (1998). https://doi.org/10.1007/BFb0055738
29. Wiener, M.: Cryptanalysis of short RSA secret exponents. IEEE Trans. Inf. Theory **36**(3), 553–558 (1990)
30. Boneh, D., Shacham, H.: Fast variants of RSA. In: RSA Laboratories' Crypto bytes. https://cseweb.ucsd.edu/~hovav/dist/survey.pdf. Accessed 4 June 2018
31. NIST: Recommendation for key management. http://nvlpubs.nist.gov/nistpubs/SpecialPublications/NIST.SP.800-57Pt3r1.pdf. Accessed 28 Nov 2017

Analysing Data Security Requirements of Android Mobile Banking Application

Shikhar Bhatnagar, Yasir Malik$^{(\boxtimes)}$, and Sergey Butakov

Department of Information Systems Security Management,
Concordia University of Edmonton, Edmonton, Canada
{sbhatna1,yasir.malik,sergey.butakov}@concordia.ab.ca

Abstract. Mobile banking applications are at high risk of cyber attacks due to security vulnerabilities in their application design and underlying operating systems. The Inter-Process Communication mechanism in Android enables applications to communicate, share data and reuse functionality between them. However, if used incorrectly, it can become an attack surface, which allows malicious applications to exploit devices and compromise sensitive financial information. In this research, we focused on addressing the intent vulnerabilities by applying a hybrid fuzzing testing technique to analyze the data security requirements of native Android financial applications. The system first automatically constructs an application behavior model and later apply hybrid fuzzing to the model to analyze the data leak vulnerabilities. Testing results help to discover the unknown exploitable entry points in the applications under test.

Keywords: Android · Intent · Fuzzing · Security testing · Data leaks

1 Introduction

Internet and Smartphone usage continues to surge rapidly, and a variety of applications and services are available for user's convenience and entertainment. Among other services, use of mobile banking is becoming common and financial companies are offering services and applications that allow its customer to carry out everyday banking ubiquitously through their mobile devices. While these services and applications greatly improve productivity, they also introduce several new risks of cyber attacks. Mobile banking applications are prone to cyber attacks due to security vulnerabilities in their application design and underlying operating systems. In the current banking application model, banks have full control over the server end, thus they have adequate measures in place to keep the data intact, but have no or little control at the user end, hence makes the user end prone to attacks.

Recently, the Android operating system has become a prime target for attackers as most of the Smartphone market is currently dominated by Android users. The Inter-Process Communication (IPC) in Android enables applications to communicate and share data and reuse functionality between them. The IPC

© Springer Nature Switzerland AG 2018
I. Traore et al. (Eds.): ISDDC 2018, LNCS 11317, pp. 30–37, 2018.
https://doi.org/10.1007/978-3-030-03712-3_3

uses intents, which is a message passing mechanism in Android, to request an action from another application component [17]. However, if used incorrectly, it could become an attack surface for exploiting exposed components and cross-application authorization, allowing malicious applications to exploit and compromise confidentiality, integrity, and availability of user's personal and financial information. In a recent Google security report, it is reported that data leakage has increased up to 10 times as compared to the previous year [9]. Attackers use evolving techniques to bypass the security mechanisms put in place by the Android to prevent user data abuse. The IPC vulnerability can also be seen as a man-in-the-middle attack in which an application that has exported component from other applications can be hijacked due to lack of permission protection to carry out the malicious task such as data leakage. This vulnerability can cause the private data to be apprehended by an unauthorized component without the user's knowledge.

The objective of this research is examining the Android communication model to analyze and verify the data security requirements of financial applications during the during IPC. We focused on addressing the intent vulnerabilities by applying a hybrid fuzzing testing technique to analyze the data security requirements of native Android financial applications. The system first automatically constructs an application behavior model and later apply hybrid fuzzing testing to the model to analyze the data leak vulnerabilities. Our testing results help to discover some unknown exploitable entry points in the applications under test. The analysis helps to improve the application data security and privacy from such vulnerabilities.

The rest of the paper is organized as follow. In Sect. 2, we present the related research work on different data security analysis techniques. The proposed approach and system description are presented in Sect. 3. Section 4 presents the discussion on experiments and results. Finally, in Sect. 5, we conclude the paper, with recommendations for future work.

2   Related Work

The OWASP[1] Mobile Application Security Verification Standard (MASVS) is a framework of security requirements to design, develop and test mobile applications [10]. The framework consists of four security verification levels, namely *L1*, *L2*, *L3*, and *L4*, where *L4* is being the topmost verification level and *L1* is the standard security which includes the list of best security practices that any mobile application should adhere to and comply with. Intents are messaging objects which are used to communicate between components of applications and to trigger the components to perform some specified action. Thus, testing these intent is very important, since intents used in application component's communication are not sanitized, and can be misused by serving as attack surface, abusing the exported components of an application to carry out attacks such as intent interception, spoofing, hijacking.

---

[1]   https://www.owasp.org/.

Numerous studies have been carried out to test the mobile banking applications against the exploited vulnerabilities [4,5,11], some notable testing techniques studied to perform application security verification of intents includes taint analysis [6,8,16], penetration and fuzzing testing [12,14,15,18]. Shezan et al. presented a study that shows, that financial applications that are registered to receive broadcast intent, such as alarm, boot completed notification, etc., can be spoofed to cause a security risk, such as data leakage, as the application would not be able to identify if component request came from system event or a malicious application [13]. A recent study shows that 33% of the financial applications that were tested, permits other applications to make changes to its files [2]. This makes financial applications vulnerable to data leakage. Similarly, Kaka et al. tested the security feature of the mobile banking application by exploiting the man-in-the-middle attack. The authors tested 19 mobile banking applications on the Android platform and observed that 90% of the applications failed to verify the origin of certificates, and even accepted third-party certificates. This led to an intrusion of the third-party entity to eavesdrop the communication between application and server [5]. In another study Kouraogo et al., tested the security of Android banking applications and banking server through reverse engineering approach. This study shows that access to the code of an application can lead to sensitive information and data of the application that can be used to apprehend the inner functioning of an application, which if misused can cause issues like a SYN flooding attack on the bank's server. There is also a possibility to repackage the banking application with malicious URLs to obtain user credentials by circulating it as a third-party application [7].

In the case of data leaks testing, studies [17,18] closely relates to our work. The authors implemented permission checking module methodology to detect ICC data leak vulnerability such as null pointer exception, intent interception, intent spoofing, intent hijacking, and data leaks. A review of literature helps us to identify some gaps that are still unsolved, such as dynamic code loading, library spoofing, activity hijacking, exception handling along with data leaks caused due to the usage of non-vetted intent communicating with exported and non-exported components. In the next section, we highlight these gaps and introduce the method to test such vulnerabilities in financial applications.

3   Data Security Analysis

This study aims to analyze the data security requirements of Android mobile banking applications during IPC by employing a hybrid fuzzing testing approach. The focus of this study is to analyze if the intents of financial applications are properly vetted, so it does not leave any security loophole to allow malicious applications to communicate through intent and exploit activity/service which is not meant to be accessible. To the best of our knowledge, the fuzzing testing technique can identify the exported services and activities, which undergo stress test yielding crash reports. This is basically caused due to programming faults, where developer unintentionally fails to implement proper exception handling and security controls.

To analyze the data flow during Inter-process communication, firstly we constructed the application behavior model using a control flow graph. Later, hybrid fuzzing was applied to the model to test the data leak vulnerabilities of financial applications during IPC exchange. Hybrid fuzzing technique includes mutation as well as generation fuzzing features, that means to implement template/seed file based on the behavior model of the target application. For mutation fuzzing, *Drozer*, an open source tool by MWR InfoSecurity is used [3]. This tool allows interacting with the underlying operating system and other applications to make use of Android Inter-Process Communication (IPC) mechanism. Some modifications were made to Drozer by adding a module named *Fuzzinozer* [1]. It is a client-side injection tool which injects intents for fuzzing testing. It provides numerous features such as broadcast intent, DOS attack, run seed, select fuzz parameters and fuzzing intent. In our analysis, we used fuzzing intent and run a seed feature for fuzzing intent functionality. While with run seed feature, manually created list of fuzzed intents were added to application components. The attributes of intent are mutated on the basis of the algorithms defined in the fuzzinozer module. The input generation method is defined for different attributes. For example, the input generator function for URI is illustrated in the code snippet 3.1, where the selection in between HTTP or HTTPS is made followed by special characters ''://'' and a random string of value between 1 and 100 is appended, followed by the domain. In the same manner, other attributes of intent are also fuzzed with respect to the generation algorithm in the module.

Code Snippet 3.1. Fuzzinozer URI input generator function [1]

```
def generate_random_uri():
return random.choice(["http", "https"]) + "://"
+ str(string_generator(random.randint(1, 100)))
+ random.choice(domains)
```

The *fuzzinozer* was used to test the financial applications and yield results like null pointer exception, illegal argument exception, and runtime exceptions. The opportunity to reuse this collected information as input motivated this study to fuzz test other components as well. The methodology is not fully automated and requires manual system training. For hybrid fuzzing testing, the methodology includes the following steps:

1. Identification of exported as well as non-exported components by statically analyzing the Android manifest file of the application.
2. Gather relevant information about intent which is fuzzable such as action and type of data, that it tends to receive through IPC by checking the intent filter. For instance, the action attribute can be fuzzed with options such as Action_Main, Action_Edit, Action_View etc., and can be used as input along with other attributes targeting the component.
3. Using information collected from the application behavior model, created null intent to test the target component identified in the first step to find the vulnerable entry point in an application.

4. Mutation test results helped to create a seed file for generative testing and intent injection to hit the target component along with the manually established number of random combinations filling up the intent attributes, i.e. ''Action'', ''Data'', ''Category'' and ''Extras'' to test data flow components.

This approach helps us to overcome the problems with current test cases in *fuzzinozer*, as it only sends the data while there is a possibility that some intents do not require/accept any data or a specific data type. Thus, the fuzzed intent ought to miss the specific component with URI and in turn, is rejected by the application. In the next section, we present results obtained by running these steps.

4 Results and Discussion

To analyze the data security requirements, experiments were conducted on 20 mobile banking and wallet applications downloaded from Google play and third-party stores. Out of which three applications were found vulnerable in improper exception handling, leaked intents and unauthorized access to activities along with data leaks and architectural security weakness.

Code Snippet 4.1. Intent leak receiver causing activity bypassing authentication

```
04-12 18:31:17.375 583   604 I ActivityManager: Displayed
net.one97.Testapp2/.wallet.activity.MoneyTransferActivity:
+1s150ms
04-12 18:31:17.821 3656 3676 W System.err:
net.one97.Testapp2.common.b.c:
{"type":null,"requestGuid":null,"orderId":null,"status":null,
"statusCode":"403","statusMessage":"Unauthorized Access",
"response":null,"metadata":null}
04-12 18:32:21.476 3656 3656 E ActivityThread:
Activity net.one97.Testapp2.wallet.activity.MoneyTransferActivity
has leaked IntentReceiver
net.one97.Testapp2.wallet.f.c$a@9492992 that was originally
registered here.
Are you missing a call to unregisterReceiver()?
04-12 18:32:21.476 3656 3656 E ActivityThread:
android.app.IntentReceiverLeaked:
Activity net.one97.Testapp2.wallet.activity.MoneyTransferActivity
has leaked IntentReceiver net.one97.Testapp2.wallet.f.c$a@9492992
```

From code snippet 4.1, it is evident that *Testapp2* leaked Intent Receiver at ''MoneyTransferActivity'', allowing unauthorized access bypassing authentication method, causing the malicious application to inject intents to target this activity and access components without any required permission. Consequently, the exploit can help the malicious application to use this activity to transfer money into different accounts without user's knowledge.

Code Snippet 4.2. Null pointer exception in Testapp2

```
12-04 17:14:17.100 5732 5732 F fuzzing_intent: type:
fuzzing package: net.one97.Testapp2 component:
net.one97.Testapp2.movies.activity.AJRCinemasSearchLanding
data_uri:http://cXxw2GJyngEL5Xad4EBuMzt5j6rrs5wKW9psqmbXWn4f.gov
category: android.intent.category.CAR_MODE
action: android.intent.action.PACKAGE_RESTARTED flag:
ACTIVITY_NO_USER_ACTION extra_type: boolean extra_key:
android.intent.extra.UID extra_value: True
--------- beginning of crash
12-04 17:14:18.223 1498 1498 E AndroidRuntime:
Process: net.one97.Testapp2, PID: 1498
--------- beginning of main
12-04 17:14:18.223 1498 1498 E AndroidRuntime:
java.lang.RuntimeException: Unable to start activity Component
Info{net.one97.Testapp2/net.one97.Testapp2.movies.activity.
AJRCinemasSearchLanding}:
java.lang.NullPointerException: Attempt to invoke
interface method 'int java.util.Map.size()' on
a null object reference
```

Code Snippet 4.3. Illegal argument exception in Testapp3

```
03-11 22:16:12.637 14431 14431 F fuzzing_intent: type:
fuzzing package: com.Testapp3 component:
com.surveymonkey.surveymonkeyandroidsdk.SMFeedbackActivity
data_uri: http://a5mOkhTgSGvkSrHQXN43DmmLXKL3wpVFhPbqQ.mil
scategory: android.intent.category.PREFERENCE action:
android.intent.action.UID_REMOVED
flag:ACTIVITY_RESET_TASK_IF_NEEDED extra_type:
boolean extra_key: android.intent.extra.ORIGINATING_URI
extra_value: False
--------- beginning of crash
03-11 22:16:15.207 11503 11503 E AndroidRuntime: FATAL EXCEPTION:
main
03-11 22:16:15.207 11503 11503 E AndroidRuntime:
Process:com.Testapp3, PID: 11503
03-11 22:16:15.207 11503 11503 E AndroidRuntime:
java.lang.RuntimeException: Unable to destroy activity
{com.Testapp3/com.surveymonkey.surveymonkeyandroidsdk.
SMFeedbackActivity}:
java.lang.IllegalArgumentException: Receiver not registered: null
```

The mutated intents injected through *Fuzzinozer* were able to detect exception handling errors, including null pointer exception, illegal argument exception, and runtime exception, leading to abnormal termination of test applications. A null pointer exception was identified in *Testapp2* which occurred due to the null object referenced to an interface method as shown in snippet 4.2. Financial application *Testapp1* crashed with intent injection on `''DeveloperConfigRcsFlagsActivity''` with the runtime exception. Financial application *Testapp3* crashed with illegal argument exception during fuzz intent injection on `''SMFeedbackActivity''` as shown in snippet 4.3. The test results show the validity of our approach that helps to identify data security vulnerabilities during the IPC. This study contributes to the data security analysis using Fuzzing approach to test components that are meant to be private, but the developer didn't assign the proper permission on the intent receiver, thus, forged intents can cause data security leakage as in the case of *Testapp2*. The analysis of financial applications concludes that the financial applications intents that carry sensitive information to communicate across application must be protected by permissions and other security controls.

5   Conclusion

In this paper, we studied the data security requirements for Android mobile banking applications and focused on addressing the Intent vulnerabilities by applying a hybrid fuzzing technique to analyze the data security requirements of native Android financial applications. A feasible solution to mitigate unauthorized access to activities through malicious intent is to sanitize the intents before an application is released for public use. Hybrid fuzzing is recommended to continuously find the vulnerabilities and improve the overall security of application including intent injection. It is also recommended that the developer of an application should put in place proper protection and authentication for application components that are marked not exported to avoid data leaks We recommend the financial applications should make the user update it to the latest version through verified application stores. This step can verify enforced certificate pinning and reduce the attacks carried out via application side loading. The prime focus of this research was to analyze the financial applications, however the same requirements apply to general purpose applications as well.

References

1. Drozer module fuzzinozer. https://github.com/mwrlabs/drozer-modules/blob/master/intents/fuzzinozer.py
2. Mobile banking applications security challenges for banks. https://www.accenture.com/t20170421T060949__w__/us-en/_acnmedia/PDF-49/Accenture-Mobile-Banking-Apps-Security-Challenges-Banks.pdf. Accessed October 2017
3. MWR infosecurity drozer tool. https://labs.mwrinfosecurity.com/tools/drozer/
4. Bojjagani, S., Sastry, V.N.: STAMBA: security testing for android mobile banking apps. In: Thampi, S., Bandyopadhyay, S., Krishnan, S., Li, K.C., Mosin, S., Ma, M. (eds.) Advances in Signal Processing and Intelligent Recognition Systems. AISC, vol. 425, pp. 671–683. Springer, Cham (2016). https://doi.org/10.1007/978-3-319-28658-7_57

5. Kaka, S., Sastry, V., Maiti, R.R.: On the MitM vulnerability in mobile banking applications for android devices. In: 2016 IEEE International Conference on Advanced Networks and Telecommunications Systems (ANTS), pp. 1–6. IEEE (2016)
6. Klieber, W., Flynn, L., Bhosale, A., Jia, L., Bauer, L.: Android taint flow analysis for app sets. In: Proceedings of the 3rd ACM SIGPLAN International Workshop on the State of the Art in Java Program Analysis, pp. 1–6. ACM (2014)
7. Kouraogo, Y., Zkik, K., Orhanou, G., et al.: Attacks on android banking applications. In: International Conference on Engineering & MIS (ICEMIS), pp. 1–6. IEEE (2016)
8. Li, L., et al.: IccTA: detecting inter-component privacy leaks in android apps. In: Proceedings of the 37th International Conference on Software Engineering-Volume 1, pp. 280–291. IEEE Press (2015)
9. Ludwig, A., Mille, M.: Diverse protections for a diverse ecosystem: Android security 2016 year in review. Google Security Blog. Google. Accessed 22 March 2017
10. Mueller, B., et al.: About the standard. Foreword by Bernhard Mueller, OWASP Mobile Project 5 Frontispiece 7 About The Standard 7 Copyright And License 7 Acknowledgements 7 (2017)
11. Panja, B., Fattaleh, D., Mercado, M., Robinson, A., Meharia, P.: Cybersecurity in banking and financial sector: security analysis of a mobile banking application. In: 2013 International Conference on Collaboration Technologies and Systems (CTS), pp. 397–403. IEEE (2013)
12. Sasnauskas, R., Regehr, J.: Intent fuzzer: crafting intents of death. In: Proceedings of the 2014 Joint International Workshop on Dynamic Analysis (WODA) and Software and System Performance Testing, Debugging, and Analytics (PERTEA), pp. 1–5. ACM (2014)
13. Shezan, F.H., Afroze, S.F., Iqbal, A.: Vulnerability detection in recent android apps: an empirical study. In: 2017 International Conference on Networking, Systems and Security (NSysS), pp. 55–63. IEEE (2017)
14. Wang, J., Chen, B., Wei, L., Liu, Y.: Skyfire: data-driven seed generation for fuzzing. In: 2017 IEEE Symposium on Security and Privacy (SP), pp. 579–594. IEEE (2017)
15. Wang, Y., Zhuge, J., Sun, D., Liu, W., Li, F.: Activityfuzzer: detecting the security vulnerabilities of android activity components
16. Wei, F., Roy, S., Ou, X., et al.: Amandroid: a precise and general inter-component data flow analysis framework for security vetting of android apps. ACM Trans. Priv. Secur. (TOPS) 21(3), 14 (2018)
17. Wu, T., Yang, Y.: Crafting intents to detect ICC vulnerabilities of android apps. In: 2016 12th International Conference on Computational Intelligence and Security (CIS), pp. 557–560. IEEE (2016)
18. Yang, K., Zhuge, J., Wang, Y., Zhou, L., Duan, H.: Intentfuzzer: detecting capability leaks of android applications. In: Proceedings of the 9th ACM symposium on Information, computer and communications security, pp. 531–536. ACM (2014)

Adaptive Mobile Keystroke Dynamic Authentication Using Ensemble Classification Methods

Faisal Alshanketi[1(✉)], Issa Traoré[1,2], Awos Kanan[2,3], and Ahmed Awad[3]

[1] ECE Department, University of Victoria, Victoria, BC, Canada
faisal_fadel2@hotmail.com, itraore@ece.uvic.ca
[2] Department of Computer Engineering, Princess Sumaya University for Technology, Amman 11941, Jordan
a.kanan@psut.edu.jo
[3] Department of School of Science, Technology, Engineering and Mathematics, University of Washington Bothell, Bothell, WA, USA
ahmeda@u.washington.edu

Abstract. Mobile keystroke dynamic biometric authentication requires several biometric samples for enrolment. In some application context or scenario where the user scarcely uses the application, it could take quite a while to get enough samples for enrolment. This creates a window of vulnerability where the user cannot be authenticated using the keystroke dynamic biometric. We propose in this paper, an adaptive approach to derive initially the user profile online and passively with a minimum number of samples, and then progressively update the profile as more samples become available. The approach uses ensemble classification methods and the equal error rate as profile maturity metric. The approach was evaluated using an existing dataset involving 42 users yielding encouraging results. The best performance achieved was an EER of 5.29% using Random forest algorithm.

Keywords: Mobile security · Keystroke dynamic biometric
Adaptive enrolment · Biometric authentication

1 Introduction

Risk-based authentication consists of determining the level of threat posed by a user by establishing how genuine the user identity is [14]. The higher the confidence in the genuineness of the user identity the lower the associated risk level, and vice-versa.

Existing risk-based authentication systems use a combination of password-based authentication, historical, and contextual information to determine the authentication risk. However, passwords are notoriously flawed: they can be broken or stolen [6]. Furthermore, contextual and historical information can be

© Springer Nature Switzerland AG 2018
I. Traoré et al. (Eds.): ISDDC 2018, LNCS 11317, pp. 38–49, 2018.
https://doi.org/10.1007/978-3-030-03712-3_4

subject to spoofing. A stronger alternative is to use biometric authentication. In this case, the authentication risk score can be derived from the biometric matching decision.

One of the main targets of authentication frauds is mobile computing because the level of security in mobile devices is in general kept to the minimum not only by design but sometimes for the convenience of the users. While different protection schemes are available on these devices, many users view these protections as hindrances, and tend to disable or bypass them [13]. In this case, security services such as risk-based authentication must be delivered in a transparent way with limited effort or expectation from the user. Some organizations are simply reluctant to require their customers to go through the process of static offline enrolment. In this situation, the profile must be built dynamically online, as more samples become available. Furthermore the profile must be updated to account the variability inherent in any behavioral biometric technology.

Behavioral biometrics such as swipe gesture and keystroke dynamics are adequate for such purpose as the biometrics can be collected transparently without the need for any special purpose sensor or any special task required from the user [11]. One of the challenges faced by such biometrics is the sparse nature of the data available. As mentioned above, for the sake of transparency, ideally enrollment must be conducted passively. This means during the enrollment phase, the authentication will have to rely on other factors, and this opens up, as a consequence, a window of vulnerability.

The objective of the research presented in this paper is to develop a model to enable user authentication in the early stage of account creation (or user registration), which typically involves reduced numbers of samples (e.g. 1, 2, or 3). However, attempting to reduce simultaneously the number of samples and the verification error rates is a difficult task since these characteristics involve trade-offs. A smaller enrollment sample set may lead to increased verification error rates.

Trade-off can be made by collecting smaller amount of data during the enrollment, which allows shortening the aforementioned window of vulnerability. While such approach is appealing, it raises the issue of profile maturity and thereby the confidence in the authentication decision being based on immature or gradually maturing profiles. Profile maturity can be improved through adaptation, by adjusting the profile based on new samples becoming available. Due to the inherent variability of behavioral biometrics, profile maturity must be improved on a regular and continuous basis, during and beyond the initial enrollment phase.

The primary goal of our research is to study profile maturity through adaptive enrollment and the confidence in such maturity. We will focus our study on extracting and analyzing keystroke dynamics for mobile devices based on fixed password authentication method.

The idea is that the user should be able to enrol initially with as little as two samples, and the profile would be upgraded gradually as more samples become available. We will determine and track confidence in the profile maturity using the Equal Error Rate (EER) as a metric [1]. The higher the confidence in the genuineness of the user identity the lower the associated risk level, and vice-versa. The approach relies on ensemble classification methods based on a basket of selected classification techniques.

The remainder of the paper is structured as follows. Section 2 provides some background information and summarizes related work. Section 3 presents our proposed adaptive authentication approach. Section 4 presents and discusses experiments results. Section 5 makes some concluding remarks.

2   Background and Related Work

In this section, we give an overview of mobile keystroke dynamics biometrics features and common performance metrics, and conduct a review of the research literature in this field.

2.1   Background on Keystroke Dynamic Biometric System

Keystroke Dynamic Features. Typing features relevant to keystroke dynamics authentication can be extracted from raw typing data obtained by measuring and analyzing various key press metric. Figure 1 depicts keystroke time information when a user presses a key down and releases it [10]. Hold time or dwell time is defined as the time for a single key press and release [15]. Flight time is the time between two consecutive key presses. Flight time and dwell time represent the most common and basic keystroke dynamic features.

Biometric System Performance. Biometric system performance is commonly measured by computing two key metrics: False Acceptance Rate (FAR) and False Rejection Rate (FRR).

FAR is the rate of falsely identifying imposter user as legitimate user which is defined as:

$$FAR = \frac{Number\ of\ false\ matches}{Total\ number\ of\ impostor\ match\ attempts}$$

FRR is the rate at which genuine users are falsely rejected from using the system which is defined as:

$$FRR = \frac{Number\ of\ false\ rejections}{Total\ number\ of\ genuine\ match\ attempts}$$

In general acceptance or rejection decisions are made by comparing the biometric matching score against some threshold value. Different values of the threshold will yield different combination of FAR/FRR. It is customary to model such variations in operating settings by using a Receiver Operating Characteristic Curve (ROC). In general, the ROC curve is defined as a plot of the false acceptance rate on the x-axis against the corresponding false rejection rate plotted on the y-axis. Another commonly used performance metric is the EER, which is defined as the value of FAR/FRR at an operating point on ROC where FAR equals FRR [12].

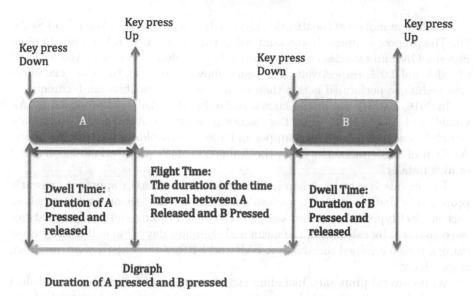

Fig. 1. Basic keystroke dynamic features.

2.2 Related Works

The first keystroke dynamic analysis for smart phones has been conducted by Clarke and Furnell in 2006 [5]. A dataset from 30 participants was collected with two different password strings typed by each participant. The first string was 11-digit phone numbers while the second string was a text message consisting of 14 words. An EER of 12.8% has been achieved using neural networks classifier on the extracted fly and dwell times features.

In 2010, Karnan and Krishnaraj [8] proposed to improve the performance of keystroke biometric authentication using genetic algorithm, Ant Colony Propagation (ACP), and Back Propagation Neural Network (BPNN). The authors collected 50 samples from 25 users using a mobile device to extract dwell and fly times. Error rates of 1.07%, 0.20%, and 0.006% were achieved using ACP, Genetic algorithms and PSO, respectively.

Another keystroke dynamic biometric authentication model has been proposed by Antal et al. [4]. In addition to the fly and dwell times, two new features were used; finger pressure and the finger area. Three anomaly detection techniques based on the Euclidean, Manhattan, and Mahalanobis distances were used [9]. The proposed model has been evaluated using a dataset collected from 42 users with each user typed the same same password (.tie5Roanl) 30 times in 2 sessions. The achieved equal error rates (EER) were 15.7%, 12.9%, and 16.6% for Euclidean, Manhattan, and Mahalanobis distances, respectively.

A different mobile authentication approach was proposed by Antal and Szabó [3]. The proposed approach was built using Bayes Network, KNN, and Random Forests. One and two-class classification using Random Forest achieved an ERR of 7.0% and 3.0%, respectively. The result shows that using two-class classification technique performed better than using one-class classification technique.

In 2016, a statistical model known as Median-Min-Diff was proposed by Al-Obaidi and Al-Jarrah [2] using the dataset provided by Antal et al. A template structure was constructed using upper and lower thresholds in the training phase. An EER of 6.79% was achieved for the evaluation of the proposed model on Antal et al.'s dataset.

The mobile keystroke dynamic biometric authentication approach, recently proposed by Jadhav et al. [7], was evaluated using a dataset of 4 subjects where each subject typed 20 password samples. Extracted timing and pressure features were analyzed by calculating the mean and standard deviation and classify users using a pre-determined threshold. A FAR and FRR of 1% and 4% were obtained, respectively.

While several proposals, including the aforementioned, have been published on mobile keystroke dynamic biometric authentication, most of these works focus on offline user enrollment, where all the samples needed are readily available. To our knowledge, limited attention has been paid on online enrolment, where the profile is built gradually and dynamically.

3   Proposed Adaptive Authentication Method

In the proposed model, we are trying to authenticate a single user while relying, at least initially, on a reduced number of collected samples. Relying on a reduced enrollment sample size allows shortening the window of vulnerability associated with the enrollment phase. While such approach is appealing, it raises the issue of profile maturity and thereby the confidence in the authentication decision based on an immature profile.

In practice, we find that it is indeed a challenging task to stay on the same classification technique to authenticate users during the training phase for long time. This is due to the fact that the performance of a classifier may fluctuate in terms of changing behavior of the user. For instance, an algorithm may achieve a very good authentication result regarding a set of training samples, but the performance may drop slightly when we get new samples over a period of time. For instance, when we start using a new password, the typing speed might change over the time until we reach a certain time where typing speed will not change any more. The problem is that the behavior of the user is changing over the time, which impacts the recognition accuracy.

To tackle the aforementioned challenge, our approach consists of using an ensemble classification scheme, involving multiple classifiers, coupled with a mechanism that aims to increase the number of samples during the training phase in an adaptive way. The mechanism will measure the performance of the system (based on the training samples) and stick with one classifier deemed as the best at the time using a specific threshold T and EER measure.

Our objective is to build a model where we can achieve a minimum acceptable EER and stay on that model based on the current training sample set. We call this approach switch and stay model.

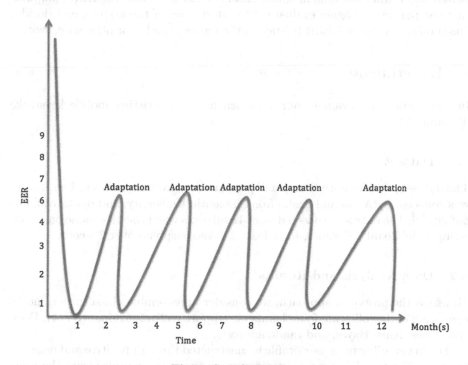

Fig. 2. Switch and stay.

In the switch and stay model, the enrollment for a given user consists of training a pool of classifiers until each classifier reaches its best performance in terms of EER on the training data. After that, we select the best classifier among the pool of classifiers. As more training samples are being added, we then stick to one classification model as long as the EER is greater than a specific threshold T. The idea is that we will stick to one model until the performance becomes unacceptable. Once the EER increases above specific threshold, the system will be retrained to reach the optimum operating point because the user behavior might change over the time and could degrade the system performance. Figure 2 depicts the switch and stay approach, where as EER fluctuates, adaptation takes place through retraining.

Figure 3 depicts the proposed system architecture. In the behaviour modelling phase, the selected model will be adapted until reaching the best performance of the system. At the same time, the classifier will be trained by using available number of samples (i.e. 1, 2, or 3 samples) to build a profile for each user. In the classifier decision phase, the EER computation component determines the best EER which achieves the lowest value of the threshold T. In the behaviour comparison phase, the selected model can be used to detect behavioural anomalies. The profile will be updated through comparing the current EER with the predefined threshold T. If EER is greater than the threshold T, then we will switch and retrain the system again. After a fixed time slot, the EER computation component will again evaluate the performance of the system, and decides based on the computed EER to stay on the current model, or otherwise, switch.

4 Experiments

In this section, we evaluate our approach using an existing mobile keystroke dynamic dataset.

4.1 Dataset

The dataset provides both timing and pressure data from keystrokes. The dataset was collected by Antal and Szabo from Sapientia University, and made available online[1] [4]. The data was collected from 42 subjects who typed the same password string ".tie5Roanl" 51 times, in at least 2 sessions spread over 2 weeks.

4.2 Data Analysis and Results

To assess the proposed approach, we consider an ensemble classification model consisting of the following four classifiers: support vector machines (SVM), Decision Trees, naïve Bayes, and random forests.

During enrollment, a user profile is constructed through positive and negative training. The training set consists of genuine (positive) samples from the users and impostor (negative) samples from other users. In practice we end up with a situation where the imposter class has more samples than the genuine class, which will generate imbalanced class distribution. To address the imbalance, we apply cost sensitive learning by assigning weights corresponding to misclassification costs to the training samples. Specifically, genuine samples are assigned greater weight compared to the impostor ones. We assign a weight P (denoted weight(P)) to the imposter class corresponding to the ratio between the total number of genuine samples and the total number of imposter samples.

---

[1] http://www.ms.sapientia.ro/~manyi/keystroke.html.

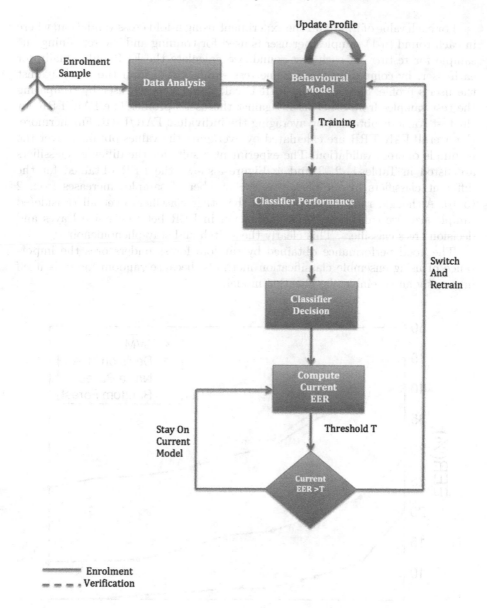

Fig. 3. Switch and StayAdaptive model.

To assess the impact of the size of the training set, we vary the number of samples per user from 2 to 10; let n denote such number ($n \geq 2$).

For each value of n, we run the experiment using n-fold cross validation, where in each round (n-1) samples per user is used for training and the remaining one sample for testing. In each test round, we calculate the FRR individually for each user, by comparing the genuine test samples (i.e. from the user) against the user's profile. Similarly, the FAR is calculated for each user by comparing the test samples from other users against the user's profile. The FAR/FRR for the test round is obtained by averaging the individual FAR/FRR. Furthermore, the overall FAR/FRR are calculated by averaging the values obtained over the n rounds of cross validation. The experiment results for the different classifiers are listed in Tables 1, 2, 3 and 4. Figure 4 shows the EER obtained for the different classifiers in our basket as the number of samples increases from 2 to 10. Although, random outperforms the other classifiers over all considered sample size, we can observe the fluctuation in EER between naive Bayes and decision trees classifiers. This clearly the switch and stay phenomenon.

The good performance obtained by random forest underscores the importance of using ensemble classification methods, because random forest is itself inherently an ensemble classification model.

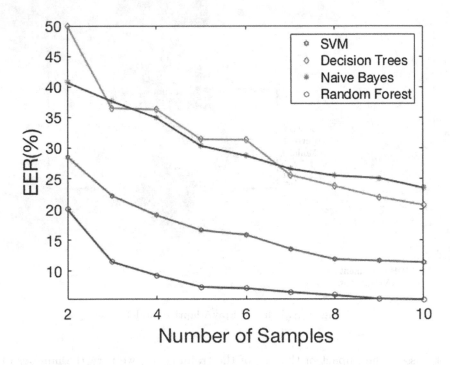

Fig. 4. EER obtained for the different when increasing the number of samples.

Table 1. Random forest performance obtained by increasing the number of samples for the same dataset.

Number of samples	Weight(P)	FRR %	FAR %
2	0.0015	21.42	19.25
3	0.00125	12.69	11.94
4	0.0011	9.52	9.80
5	0.00104	7.61	7.24
6	0.0010	7.53	7.10
7	0.00095	7.14	7.19
8	0.0009	6.54	6.42
9	0.00088	6.08	6.08
10	0.00086	5.23	5.35

Table 2. SVM performance obtained by increasing the number of samples for the same dataset.

Number of samples	Weight(P)	FRR %	FAR %
2	0.014	28.57	29.35
3	0.019	22.22	21.58
4	0.020	19.04	19.54
5	0.025	16.6	16.92
6	0.028	15.87	15.30
7	0.032	13.60	13.76
8	0.036	11.90	11.38
9	0.035	11.64	11.87
10	0.036	11.42	11.46

Table 3. Decision trees performance obtained by increasing the number of samples for the same dataset.

Number of samples	Weight(P)	FRR %	FAR %
2	0.035	100	0
3	0.035	36.50	24.69
4	0.0176	36.30	36.70
5	0.0143	31.42	31.95
6	0.0135	31.34	30.08
7	0.017	25.58	26.28
8	0.017	23.80	23.51
9	0.017	21.95	22.21
10	0.016	20.71	20.30

Table 4. Naive Bayes performance obtained by increasing the number of samples for the same dataset.

Number of samples	Weight(P)	FRR %	FAR %
2	0.0246	40.47	40.96
3	0.0246	38.09	37.22
4	0.0246	35.71	34.20
5	0.025	30.47	30.19
6	0.025	28.17	29.29
7	0.0254	26.53	26.46
8	0.0254	25.0	25.99
9	0.0254	25.13	25.02
10	0.0255	23.09	23.90

5 Conclusion

With the progress achieved to this date in mobile computing technologies, mobile devices are increasingly being used to store sensitive data and perform security-critical transactions and services. However, the protection available on these devices is still lagging behind. The primary and often only protection mechanism in these devices is authentication using a password or a PIN. Passwords are notoriously known to be a weak authentication mechanism, no matter how complex the underlying format is. Mobile authentication can be strengthened by extracting and analyzing keystroke dynamic biometric from supplied passwords.

Although keystroke dynamics biometric techniques can achieve high accuracy rates for larger amount of data during the enrollment, it is still challenging to identify a subject for smaller amount of data during the enrollment. We have presented in this paper a method to verify the subject for minimum dataset available (e.g. 1, 2, 3 or minimum samples). The approach uses ensemble classification and tracks profile maturity using the EER. Experimental evaluation using an existing dataset indicates the feasibility of the proposed approach.

In the experiments presented in this paper, we used only four classifiers in our basket. Our future work will consist of investigating a much larger pool of classifiers.

Our future work will also investigate keystroke dynamic biometric extracted from One-Time Password (OTP). Despite the biometric factor, using fixed password strings can be vulnerable to replay attacks. A sophisticated key logger can be implemented to sniff the password strings along with keystroke dynamics, which can then be reused to gain access to the protected system. One approach to mitigate such threat, is to extract the keystroke dynamics from OTP. This approach still poses significant challenges in terms of accuracy.

Acknowledgment. This research is supported by the Jazan University and the Ministry of Education of the Kingdom of Saudi Arabia.

References

1. Ahmed, A.A., Traore, I.: Biometric recognition based on free-text keystroke dynamics. IEEE Trans. Cybern. **44**(4), 458–472 (2014)
2. Al-Obaidi, N.M., Al-Jarrah, M.M.: Statistical median-based classifier model for keystroke dynamics on mobile devices. In: 2016 Sixth International Conference on Digital Information Processing and Communications (ICDIPC), pp. 186–191, April 2016
3. Antal, M., Szabó, L.Z.: An evaluation of one-class and two-class classification algorithms for keystroke dynamics authentication on mobile devices. In: 2015 20th International Conference on Control Systems and Computer Science, pp. 343–350, May 2015
4. Antal, M., Szabó, L.Z., László, I.: Keystroke dynamics on android platform. Procedia Technol. **19**, 820–826 (2015)
5. Clarke, N.L., Furnell, S.M.: Authenticating mobile phone users using keystroke analysis. Int. J. Inf. Secur. **6**(1), 1–14 (2006)
6. El-Abed, M., Dafer, M., El Khayat, R.: RHU keystroke: a mobile-based benchmark for keystroke dynamics systems. In: Proceedings of the 48th IEEE International Carnahan Conference on Security Technology (2012)
7. Jadhav, C., Kulkami, S., Shelar, S., Shinde, K., Dharwadkar, N.V.: Biometrie authentication using keystroke dynamics. In: 2017 International Conference on I-SMAC (IoT in Social, Mobile, Analytics and Cloud) (I-SMAC), pp. 870–875, February 2017
8. Karnan, M., Krishnaraj, N.: Keystroke dynamic approach to secure mobile devices. In: 2010 IEEE International Conference on Computational Intelligence and Computing Research (ICCIC), pp. 1–4, December 2010
9. Killourhy, K.S., Maxion, R.A.: Comparing anomaly-detection algorithms for keystroke dynamics. In: IEEE/IFIP International Conference on Dependable Systems Networks, DSN 2009, pp. 125–134, June 2009
10. Leggett, J., Williams, G., Usnick, M., Longnecker, M.: Dynamic identity verification via keystroke characteristics. Int. J. Man-Mach. Stud. **35**(6), 859–870 (1991)
11. Neal, T.J., Woodard, D.L.: Surveying biometric authentication for mobile device security. J. Pattern Recogn. Res. **1**, 74–110 (2016)
12. Pankanti, S., Ratha, N.K., Bolle, R.M.: Structure in errors: a case study in fingerprint verification. In: Object Recognition Supported by User Interaction for Service Robots (2002)
13. Woodard, D., Banerjee, S.P.: Biometric authentication and identification using keystroke dynamics: a survey. J. Pattern Recogn. Res. **7**(1), 116–139 (2012)
14. Shanmugapriya, D., Padmavathi, G.: A survey of biometric keystroke dynamics: approaches, security and challenges. arXiv preprint arXiv:0910.0817 (2009)
15. Stefan, D., Yao, D.D.: Keystroke-dynamics authentication against synthetic forgeries. In: 2010 6th International Conference on Collaborative Computing: Networking, Applications and Worksharing (CollaborateCom), pp. 1–8. IEEE (2010)

Automating Incident Classification Using Sentiment Analysis and Machine Learning

Marina Danchovsky Ibrishimova[✉] and Kin Fun Li

University of Victoria, Victoria, BC, Canada
{marinaibrishimova, kinli}@uvic.ca

Abstract. The first step in an incident response plan of an organization is to establish whether the reported event is in fact an incident. This is not an easy task especially if it is a novel event, which has not previously been documented. A typical classification of a novel event includes consulting a database of events with similar keywords and making a subjective decision by human. Efforts have been made to categorize events but there is no universal list of all possible incidents because each incident can be described in multiple different ways. In this paper we propose automating the process of receiving and classifying an event based on the assumption that the main difference between an event and an incident in the field of security is that an event is a positive or a neutral occurrence whereas an incident has strictly negative connotations. We applied sentiment analysis on event reports from the RISI dataset, and the results supported our assumption. We further observed that the sentiment analysis score and magnitude parameters of similar incidents were also very similar and we used them as features in a machine learning model along with other features obtained from each report such as impact and duration in order to predict the likelihood that an event is an incident. We found that using sentiment analysis as a feature of the model increases its accuracy, precision, and recall by at least 10%. The difference between our approach and the typical incident classification approach is that in our approach we train the system to recognize the incidents before any incident actually takes place and our system can recognize incidents even if their descriptions do not include keywords previously encountered by the system.

Keywords: Incident response classification · Machine learning
Natural language processing · Security · Sentiment analysis

1 Introduction

A typical security event classification process involves gathering information about what type of an event has occurred, how many people and systems the event has affected, whether the event was an attack on the confidentiality, integrity, or availability of data, systems, and services, and whether any laws or business contracts were being violated. Traditionally, someone would have to fill out a form with this information and submit it to a help desk employee. Subsequently, the employee would try to classify the event by comparing it to other incidents. If the employee has trouble establishing the severity of the event, then they would typically consult other sources before making a

© Springer Nature Switzerland AG 2018
I. Traore et al. (Eds.): ISDDC 2018, LNCS 11317, pp. 50–62, 2018.
https://doi.org/10.1007/978-3-030-03712-3_5

final decision on how to classify the incident including consulting a database of security incidents and/or discussing the incident with a more senior employee. This could take time and time is of essence in an emergency situation [1, 2].

Automation can be used in order to speed up the process of incident classification. Efforts have been made to standardize the language used in security incident reports but the sheer complexity of human language has been a major roadblock in such efforts [3]. A standardized taxonomy of incident terms is required in order to automate the process of incident classification using pattern matching but then those who report the incident must know and use the exact same keywords as the ones in the taxonomy because pure pattern matching algorithms can not recognize synonyms and similar phrases. In essence, automating incident classification using pattern matching is not the optimal solution because there are many different ways in which an event can be described and so the taxonomy would have to accommodate for this. In addition, human language is not static and as new words related to security incidents emerge they would have to be added to the taxonomy. Thus the taxonomy would keep growing and the time to traverse it would keep growing as well.

In this paper we evaluate an alternative approach, which is based on the observation that the term "event" has either a positive or a neutral sentiment whereas the term "incident" has a strictly negative sentiment. We propose automating the process of incident classification in a system that uses sentiment analysis on the description of the event as features in a logistic regression machine learning model in order to make a prediction on the likelihood that the event is an incident. The other features of the model are ternary features related to the event impact on the confidentiality, integrity, or availability of data and services, the event scope of the affected units, and a binary feature related to the reliability of the source of the report. The machine learning model is trained and saved before the system goes live on a dataset of incidents and events. Once the system goes live and starts receiving incident reports the model quickly determines the probability that an event is an incident based on the information in the report. The report consists of the event description, and questions related to the scope and impact. The questions are typical of security reports but in our model they only have ternary answers, namely yes, no, and unknown. We used a genetic algorithm to determine whether the sentiment score and magnitude features improve the model's learning or whether the typical questions asked in a report are sufficient to achieve good accuracy, precision and recall without the need of sentiment analysis and we describe our findings in Sect. 4 of this paper.

Our motivation for this system is to make the process of incident classification faster and more efficient. The traditional approach of classifying a cyber event is described in Sect. 2. Our proposed system is introduced in Sect. 3. Our findings are presented in Sect. 4. A comparison between the traditional typical approach and our automated approach is made in Sect. 5. Finally, conclusions are made in Sect. 6.

2 The Typical Approach

The typical approach of incident classification involves constructing and referring to a dictionary of common terms. Different organizations have different dictionaries and there are no common set of phrases to describe possible security events, which are adopted universally. This makes the job of classifying an incident very difficult [3]. The only events that can be immediately classified with great certainty using the typical approach are events with keywords that appear in the dictionary of common terms of a particular organization.

Figure 1. describes a typical event classification process that involves a human employee. As Fig. 1 suggests, the help desk employee could easily get stuck on trying to identify whether a particular event is in fact an incident especially if the employee hasn't had much experience classifying security incidents before or if the event does not contain known keywords. The same issues arise if the event classification process is automated using a pattern matching algorithm. Both of these approaches require a universal set of words and phrases to describe security events.

As discussed in [3] the main ways in which people have tried to create a universal set of terms is by using one of the following techniques:

1. Results categories - how the event affects processes
2. List(s) of categories - list all types of possible attacks
3. Action categories - categories based on what the event is

A case study in [1] defines 3 results categories based on how the events in these categories affect the fundamental aspects of security. These fundamental aspects known as the CIA triad are confidentiality (or secrecy as the author in [1] puts it), integrity, and availability. Whether an event could escalate into an incident does depend on factors such as whether it can cause disruption to the availability of systems and services, or whether it compromises the integrity and confidentiality of data. Unfortunately, some events that are incidents might not attack the CIA triad. For example, an employee clicking on a potentially malicious link at work does not affect the availability, integrity, or confidentiality of systems by itself but it still can be considered an incident depending on the company policy and whether the link is actually malicious or not. Another example involves unconfirmed events: if the source of the report cannot prove that the event took place then event is not an incident even if it attacks the CIA triad [7].

Another approach is to compile and use a list of categories as described in [4]. The list contains 94 different types of attacks. Although the list seems inexhaustible, it appears that all incidents share one thing in common: they are all negative occurrences. Furthermore, we examined each of these theoretical attack types and the real life incidents compiled in RISI dataset and we noticed a pattern that confirms the obser-vations made in [3]. Namely, there are certain action words associated with security events. Unfortunately, the list of action words described in [3] is not complete. Actions such as leak and deny are not covered under the proposed set of action words in [3]. However, these words do appear very often in real life datasets such as the dataset in [6]. In addition, some of these action words can be nouns as well. The verb "access" by

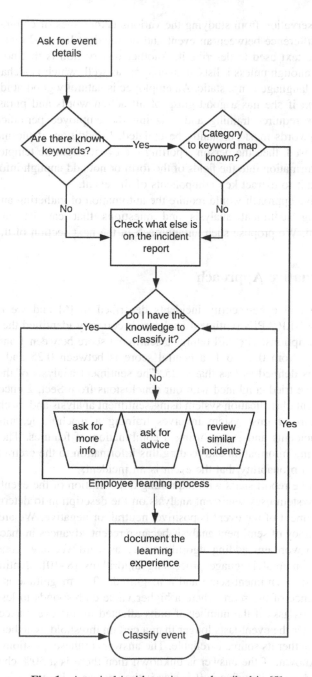

Fig. 1. A typical incident triage as described in [5]

itself has a neutral sentiment but the phrase "unauthorized access" has a strictly negative sentiment. The adjective "unauthorized" is modifying the action noun "access". Clearly, certain linguistic components can alter the overall sentiment of a phrase.

The key observation from studying the various taxonomies of common phrases is that the main difference between an event and an incident has to do with the overall sentiment of the text used to describe it. Another observation is that no taxonomy is comprehensive enough unless it lists all synonyms as well, which is a challenging task because human language is not static. An employee is naturally good at identifying the sentiment of text if she has a good grasp of all action words and phrases *and* their synonyms. This requires training and quizzing the employee periodically and the database of keywords must constantly be updated. In addition, if the incident report form is paper-based, then the person reporting the event might be tempted to provide unnecessary information into the fields of the form or not add enough information thus making it difficult to extract key components of the event.

An alternative approach would require the automation of gathering and identifying the event using sentiment analysis and questions that can be answered with yes/no/unknown. We propose such an approach in the next section of this paper.

3   An Alternative Approach

We studied 30 real cybersecurity incidents described in [6] and we ran each one through Google NLP API's sentiment analysis. It correctly identified the sentiment of all incident descriptions. The API returns a sentiment score between 1 and −1 where a positive score is from 0.25 to 1, a neutral score is between 0.25 and −0.25 and a negative score is defined as less than 0.25. The sentiment analysis of these examples and the others we tried combined with our conclusions from Sect. 2 encouraged us to design an incident classification system using sentiment analysis and machine learning.

The first part of this system involves training a machine learning model on examples of incidents and events using a combination of features. The second part involves gathering information and feeding this information to the pretrained model in order to obtain a probability that the event is an incident.

The interactive report starts with requesting a description of the event as described in Fig. 2. The system uses sentiment analysis on the description to determine whether the overall sentiment of the event is positive, neutral, or negative. We are confident in the overall accuracy of sentiment analysis because recent advances in machine learning and in particular word embedding algorithms such as word2vec have greatly improved the accuracy of natural language processing algorithms [8–10]. Sentiment analysis returns 2 values: a sentiment score and a magnitude. The magnitude is basically the level of confidence of the score where a higher value corresponds to less confidence. Next, our systems asks if the number of units affected by the event exceeds a certain threshold, whether the event lasts longer than a certain threshold, whether it attacks the CIA triad, or whether its source is reliable. The answers to these questions can be either yes, no, or unknown. If the answer is unknown then there is a 50% chance that it is either a yes or a no so its value is 0.5, else if the answer is known it is 1 or 0.

```
State the nature of the event.
A European utility reported that a virus attacked their Distribution SCADA system
Sentiment: -0.699999988079071, 0.699999988079071
Is the event an attack on the confidentiality, integrity, or availability?
yes
Does the event affect more than one person and/or unit?
yes
Can you prove that the event took place?
yes
The probability that the event is an incident is:
[0.70528466]
```

Fig. 2. Gathering the event report: a screenshot from our program

After gathering the event report, the system feeds the data as an unlabeled example into a trained and saved logistic regression machine learning model. Its prediction function is then used to retrieve a percentage of the likelihood that an event is an incident. This model should be pretrained on a dataset composed of incidents combined with reports of regular computer events. The description of each example of this dataset must be fed through a sentiment analysis tool to obtain values for the sentiment score and its magnitude. A sample of labeled examples is shown in Fig. 3 and an overview of the entire automated system is described in Fig. 4.

Features						Label
Description Score	Description Magnitude	Does it affect more than x? y/n/unknown	Does it last more than y? y/n/unknown	Does it attack the CIA triad? y/n/unknown	Is it confirmed? y/n	Is it incident
-0.7	0.7	1.0	1.0	1.0	1.0	1.0
-0.3	1.0	0	0	0.5	0	0
-0.4	0.8	1.0	0.5	1.0	1.0	1.0
-0.5	0.5	1.0	0	1.0	1.0	1.0
0.2	0.2	0.5	0	0	0	0

Fig. 3. A sample of labeled examples

In our code we use a logistic regression model as a binary classifier that always ensures an output between 0 and 1 because it utilizes the Sigmoid function as shown in Fig. 5 [11]. This enables our model to return a probability between 0 and 1 of how likely it is that an event is in fact an incident. In particular, we use TensorFlow's LinearClassifier, which is a regression model for classification tasks as described in [16]. Since we are dealing with two distinct binary classes, namely an event and an

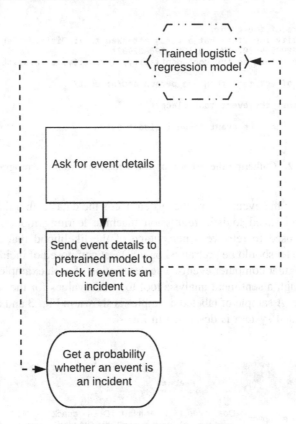

Fig. 4. Our proposed system

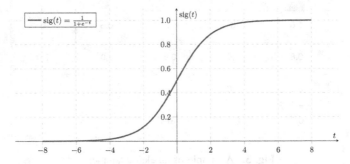

Fig. 5. The Sigmoid function ensures that the logistic regression model always returns a target value between 0 and 1 [11].

incident, then we need this particular model with a classification threshold in order to better distinguish between the two events especially because different organizations have different tolerance levels for what constitutes an incident.

4 Result Analysis

In order to verify the accuracy of our model, we gathered a dataset of examples of incidents and regular events described in [6] and [7]. For each example we obtained 6 features. The first two features are sentiment score and magnitude, which we obtained using Google Natural Language Processing API. The other 4 features are all associated with ternary answers to questions related to the event, namely whether the event affects more than x people, whether it lasts more than y minutes, whether it attacks the confidentiality, integrity, or availability of resources, and whether the source of the report can prove that the event took place. We assigned a score of 1.0 if the answer to any of these questions was true, 0 if it was false. We assign 0.5 if the answer is unknown since in this case the probability of the answer being true or false is 50%. For each example's target or label we assign a value of 1 or 0 based on whether the event comes from [6], which is a dataset of incidents or [9] which contains examples of regular events that are not incidents. Our original dataset consists of 10 such incidents and 10 such events. We generated a synthetic dataset with 20000 labeled examples with the same distribution as the original dataset using Python's numpy choice function. 12000 of these examples are being used to train the model and the remaining 8000 examples are used to test and validate the model.

We used a Genetic Algorithm (GA) to determine what is the optimal number of features, which is possible because our search space is rather small. We also wanted to find out whether sentiment analysis improves the model's learning at all. Genetic algorithms appear to be superior to other search-based algorithms for feature selection at a higher computational cost [15] but since the search space in our case consists of only 32 possible solutions, then the computational cost is not an issue since it would take at most 32 iterations to either find a solution or terminate.

We used binary encoding to map each solution to a binary vector. Each bit (gene) in an individual solution (chromosome) represents whether or not the corresponding feature has been included in the solution. Figure 6 describes a sample of solutions along with the values used for the fitness function of our GA. The GA's fitness function is the model's accuracy, precision, and recall on the validation examples for a particular combination of features. Each combination represents a unique solution.

In order to obtain the fitness of each solution, we ran each solution through our logistic regression model and we retrieved the metrics used to evaluate the model's learning, namely the accuracy, precision, and recall for the 8000 validation examples. Accuracy is calculated by dividing the total number of predictions by the number of correct predictions, Precision measures "what proportion of all positive identifications was identified correctly" and recall represents "what proportion of actual positives was identified correctly" [12]. In machine learning, if the accuracy, precision, and recall of model A are higher the accuracy, precision, and recall of model B then model A is better than model B [12].

Figure 7 shows the mathematical descriptions of these metrics. The solution with the highest accuracy, precision and recall is the optimal solution to our problem. As described in Fig. 6, the first solution we ran did not include the sentiment score and magnitude features. This solution yielded the lowest accuracy, precision, and recall at 73%, 72%, and 84% respectively. The next solution we ran included only the sentiment score and magnitude features. This solution did much better with accuracy, precision, and recall at 86%, 85%, and 91% respectively. The optimal solution is Solution #4, which included 5 out of the 6 possible features we extracted from our datasets of events, namely the score, the magnitude, whether the event affects more than x, whether it attacks the CIA triad, and whether it is confirmed (i.e. the source is reliable or not). After choosing the best combination of features for the model we then trained it using 12000 training examples, tested it out using 8000 validation examples, and saved it so that it is ready to make unlabeled predictions on whether an event is an incident or not. Note that the grid in Fig. 6 can be tailored to the specific requirements of any organization.

		Features					
		Feat #1	Feat #2	Feat #3	Feat #4	Feat #5	Feat #6
Solutions & Fitness		Score	Magni-tude	Affects more than x?	Lasts more than y?	Attacks CIA triad?	Is source reliable?
Sol. #1	Accuracy: 73% Precision: 72% Recall: 84%	0	0	1	1	1	1
Sol. #2	Accuracy: 86% Precision: 85% Recall: 91%	1	1	0	0	0	0
Sol. #3	Accuracy: 95% Precision: 92% Recall: 99%	1	1	1	0	0	0
Sol. #4	Accuracy: 96% Precision: 97% Recall: 99%	1	1	1	0	1	1
Sol. #5	Accuracy: 96% Precision: 93% Recall: 99%	1	1	1	1	1	1

Fig. 6. A sample of solutions representing combinations of features used to train our logistic regression model.

$$\text{Accuracy} = \frac{\text{number of correct predictions}}{\text{total number of predictions}}$$

$$= \frac{TP + TN}{TP + TN + FP + FN}$$

where TP = True Positives, TN = True Negatives,
FP = False Positives, and FN = False Negatives

$$\text{Precision} = \frac{TP}{TP + FP}$$

$$\text{Recall} = \frac{TP}{TP + FN}$$

Fig. 7. The equations for the metrics used in evaluating the logistic regression model.

In summary, the prototype we built is composed of 3 modules.

1. The first module has the following functions:
   a. g(n) generates a larger dataset from a sample dataset of events using Python's numpy choice function. (only needed if a large dataset is not present)
   b. f(n) transforms the features of the dataset into the proper format that GA can use. (Only needed to verify the fitness of different combinations of features as proposed in this paper)
   c. h(n) evaluates the fitness of different combinations of features using a GA (only needed for the initial feature selection).
2. The second module contains a linear regression model as described in [11], which is configured to work best with our dataset in terms of different parameters such as learning rate, batch size, and so on. These configurations are expected to work for other datasets with an identical structure as the dataset described in this paper.
3. The third module contains the interactive incident report form, which is needed to obtain information about the event by
   a. Asking for the event description and running this description through a natural language processing API in order to obtain a sentiment analysis score and magnitude, which are the first two features that the model needs in order to make a prediction on whether the event is an incident or not.
   b. Asking if it is known whether the event affects more than a certain number of units, whether it attacks the confidentiality, or integrity, or availability of data and services, and whether the event can be confirmed or not. These are the last 3 features the model needs in order to make a prediction on whether the event is an incident or not.
   c. Feeding the collected features to the model, which returns a probability that the event is an incident.

In both the typical approach and our approach an incident report is needed before a classification can be made. We designed an interactive incident response chatbot to gather the incident report. In real time it obtains a description of the event and then it runs this description through Google NLP API in order to get sentiment score and magnitude of the event. It further obtains the likelihood that the event affects more than x, that it attacks the CIA triad, and that its source is reliable. It then sends these details to the saved model, which returns a probability that the event is an incident. Our model has a recall of 99%. In other words, it correctly identifies if an event is an incident 99% of the time.

5 Comparing the Human and Machine Approaches

The main difference between the approach we describe in Sect. 3 of this paper and the typical approach described in Sect. 2 is that in the typical approach the process of learning how to classify a novel event, which does not contain known keywords, happens while the event is being reported. This can be clearly seen in Fig. 1. Additional information must be gathered on the spot from various sources, which can cause a delay in the classification of the event. Time is of essence in an emergency situation and the typical approach can take a long time before a final decision is made. In contrast, our approach pre-trains the system to recognize when an event is likely an incident as described in Fig. 8. In addition, our approach does not require the keyword memorization and pattern matching processes described in the typical approach. In fact, our system can correctly identify incidents even if they contain keywords never encountered by the system.

The typical approach requires employees to review each report and these employees must analyze and process incoming reports in real time therefore they must be available as long as the organization's network is available. An automated system is always present when the organization's network is available. The model training is done only once and modern GPUs can do it very efficiently [13]. For example, GeForce 1070 can process 6000–7000 training examples per second so the entire training of the model can be done in just a few seconds depending on the GPU [14]. Figure 8 shows performance benchmarks of different GPUs as shown in [14].

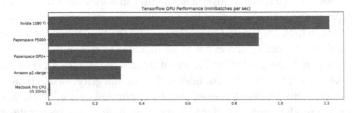

Fig. 8. Tensorflow Performance Benchmarks for different GPUs. This figure was taken from [14]

Once the training is done, making a prediction on an unlabeled example takes less than a millisecond. The sentiment analysis of an event description that has 500 words or less takes less than a second using Google NLP API.

6 Conclusion

We present a fully automated incident classification system, which analyses user input to extract information pertaining to whether the event is an incident or not. Rather than preprogramming how it should deal with particular events, it acquires the ability to classify events using machine learning and natural language processing. In particular, it applies sentiment analysis to the event description to establish whether it is a positive, negative, or neutral event. In information security the key difference between an event and an incident is that an incident is a strictly negative situation whereas an event is either positive or neutral. The system uses a logistic regression model to predict whether the event is an incident or not based on the user input and the analysis conducted by the NLP algorithm. A machine learning model is only as good as the data used to train it. Unfortunately, since incident response is a sensitive topic, it is difficult to find publicly available data other than the data described in [6].

Currently we are experimenting with various feature selection approaches and training models. Also, we are investigating whether the proper generation of a large synthetic dataset is worth pursuing and whether it is beneficial to the security research community if the dataset is made publicly available.

References

1. Cohen, F.B.: Protection and Security on the Information Superhighway. Wiley, New York (1995)
2. ITU-T X.1056 Recommendations. http://handle.itu.int/11.1002/1000/9615. Accessed 02 June 2018
3. Howard, J.D., Longstaff, T.A.: A common language for computer security incidents. United States (1998). https://doi.org/10.2172/751004
4. Cohen, F.: Information system attacks: a preliminary classification scheme. Comput. Secur. **16**(1), 29–46 (1997)
5. AI Automation for incident management. https://medium.com/kmeanswhat/ai-automation-for-incident-management-c872ee10e833. Accessed 02 June 2018
6. http://www.risidata.com/Database/P30. Accessed 02 June 2018
7. Pham, C.: From events to incidents, SANS InfoSec Reading Room. https://www.sans.org/reading-room/whitepapers/incident/events-incidents-646. Accessed 02 June 2018
8. Mikolov, T., Chen, K., Corrado, G., Dean, J.: Efficient Estimation of Word Representations in Vector Space. CoRR, abs/1301.3781 (2013)
9. Mikolov, T., Sutskever, I., Chen, K., Corrado, G., Dean, J.: Distributed representations of words and phrases and their compositionality. In: Burges, C.J.C., Bottou, L., Welling, M., Ghahramani, Z., Weinberger, K.Q. (eds.) Proceedings of the 26th International Conference on Neural Information Processing Systems, (NIPS 2013), vol. 2, pp. 3111–3119. Curran Associates Inc., USA (2013)

10. Bae, S., Yi, Y.: Acceleration of Word2vec using GPUs. In: Hirose, A., Ozawa, S., Doya, K., Ikeda, K., Lee, M., Liu, D. (eds.) ICONIP 2016. LNCS, vol. 9948, pp. 269–279. Springer, Cham (2016). https://doi.org/10.1007/978-3-319-46672-9_31
11. Logistic Regression: Calculating a probability. https://developers.google.com/machine-learning/crash-course/logistic-regression/calculating-a-probability. Accessed 02 June 2018
12. Classification: precision and recall. https://developers.google.com/machine-learning/crash-course/classification/precision-and-recall. Accessed 02 June 2018
13. Lazorenko, A.: TensorFlow Performance Test: CPU vs GPU. https://medium.com/andriyl azorenko/tensorflow-performance-test-cpu-vs-gpu-79fcd39170c. Accessed 02 June 2018
14. Chu, V.: Benchmarking Tensorflow Performance and Cost Across Different GPU Options. https://medium.com/initialized-capital/benchmarking-tensorflow-performance-and-cost-across-different-gpu-options-69bd85fe5d58. Accessed 02 June 2018
15. Vafaie, H., Imam, I.F.: Feature selection methods: genetic algorithms vs. greedy-like search. In: Proceedings of the 3rd International Fuzzy Systems and Intelligent Control Conference, Louisville, KY, March 1994
16. LinearClassifier. https://www.tensorflow.org/api_docs/python/tf/estimator/LinearClassifier. Accessed 12 June 2018

Security Analysis of an Identity-Based Data Aggregation Protocol for the Smart Grid

Zhiwei Wang[✉], Hao Xie, and Yumin Xu

Nanjing University of Posts and Telecommunications,
Nanjing 210023, Jiangsu, China
zhwwang@njupt.edu.cn

Abstract. Recently, Wang et al. proposed an efficient identity-based aggregation protocol for the smart grid, and they proved the cryptographic primitives used in protocol formally. However, they did not use a formal methodology for evaluating their security or privacy guarantees, especially for resisting the colluding attacks. In this paper, we provide a formal security and privacy definitions for the identity-based data aggregation protocol. When we applied the security definitions for Wang et al.'s protocol, we find that this protocol can resist two kinds of colluding attacks, but it can be broken by the other three kinds of colluding attacks. Thus, this protocol is not secure in practical. Our analysis methodology also can be used for other data aggregation protocols, and it is beneficial for the protocol designers.

Keywords: Aggregation protocol · Identity-based encryption
Colluding attacks · Formal methodology

1 Introduction

Compared with traditional power grid, smart gird brings significant improvement on the reliability, flexibility, security, efficiency and load adjustment/load balancing of electric system [1,2]. For some use cases in smart grid, e.g., price forecasting and load balancing, the total power usage data of a area, e.g., a city or a neighbourhood is needed for the electricity service provider (ESP) [9]. In one area, there exists a collector as a bridge between the ESP and the smart meters. It sends the aggregated power usage data to its ESP, and the ESP can only obtain the total power consumption data, as Fig. 1. However, the individual consumption values of each meters may leak the privacy information of customers, including daily activities. Thus, a large number of secure and privacy-preserving aggregation protocols have been proposed [3–8].

Recently, Wang et al. presented an identity-based data aggregation protocol for the smart grid [6], which uses a homomorphic identity-based encryption scheme to aggregate the data, and utilizes an identity-based signature scheme

© Springer Nature Switzerland AG 2018
I. Traore et al. (Eds.): ISDDC 2018, LNCS 11317, pp. 63–73, 2018.
https://doi.org/10.1007/978-3-030-03712-3_6

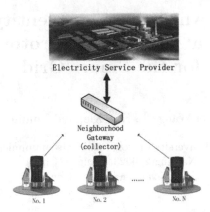

Fig. 1. Metering data aggregation protocol

with batch verification to protect the ciphertexts of metering data. They proved the cryptographic primitives in their protocol, and analysis the protocol in six typical attacks in smart grid. However, they do not provide a formal methodology for evaluating the security and privacy of the protocol [10–12]. In the smart grid, the ESPs, the collectors and the smart meters are all possibly controlled by an attacker, and they can collude to attack the honest meters, e.g., retrieving the consumption data of an honest smart meter or determining which metering data is associated with an honest smart meter. Thus, the goal of us is to present a formal security and privacy analysis to Wang et al.'s protocol against the colluding attacks.

In this paper, we firstly propose formal definitions of CPA security and unlinkability of identity-based aggregation protocols, and then we use the formal methodology to analysis Wang et al.'s protocol [6] against five typical colluding attacks. Among these five attacks, three attacks of them are to break the CPA security, while two attacks of them are to break the unlinkability. From analysis, we find that Wang et al.'s protocol [6] can only resists two colluding attacks.

This paper is organized as follows. In Sect. 2, we describe the definitions of CPA security and unlinkability. In Sect. 3, we review Wang et al.'s identity-based data aggregation protocol. In Sect. 4, we present formal security analysis for Wang's Protocol against five colluding attacks. In Sect. 5, we draw the conclusion.

2   Security Definition

In identity-based data aggregation protocol, the security concern is to keep the confidentiality of individual metering data of smart meters, while the privacy concern is to let the ESP only learn the sum of metering data. In this paper, security and privacy are only concerned in terms of recovering the individual plaintexts of each smart meters, and other security guarantees of identity-based aggregation protocol against malicious parties are out of the scope of this paper.

We model the chosen plaintext attack security [13] of individual data of smart meters in the form of a game called *CPA security game of smart meters*, while model the unlinkability of individual data of smart meters in the form of a game called *unlinkability game of smart meters*. These two games are played between two parties called *challenger* and *attacker*, where the challenger controlling the parties that concern their security and privacy acts honestly, and attacker controlling the parties that violates the CPA security and privacy objective of smart meters. The attacker is assumed to have all the secret information of the parties under its control, so as the challenger.

In CPA security game, the number of dishonest smart meters is $N-1$ meaning all but one smart meter are dishonest, and attacker want to retrieve the consumption of the single honest smart meter. In unlinkability game, the number of dishonest smart meters is limited to $N-2$, that means at least two smart meters, SM_i and SM_j, are honest, where $1 \leq i, j \leq N$. The definition of unlinkability means that even the attacker knows the individual metering data of these two honest smart meters, it still cannot known which metering data are associated with SM_i or SM_j after the protocol has been executed. In the attacker failures in CPA security game or unlinkability game, then it indicates the CPA security or privacy of this protocol is against the consumed colluding set(s).

Formally, the **CPA security game of smart meters** for identity-based data aggregation protocol is defined as follows:

1. The initialization and registration phases of identity-based data aggregation protocol is run, and the attacker gets the identity and other public parameters.
2. The attacker outputs two metering plaintexts m_0 and m_1 with the same length.
3. The challenger chooses a random bit $b \in \{0, 1\}$, and assigns m_b as the metering data for the only one honest smart meter. And then, it encrypts m_b by using the private key, where the ciphertext is the challenging ciphertext.
4. The remain parts of protocol are executed, and the attacker want to determine b.
5. Finally, the attacker outputs a guess bit b'. If $b = b'$, then it wins the game, and the output of this game is denoted as 1, and 0 otherwise.

If the attacker only has a negligible winning probability in the above game, then we say the identity-based data aggregation protocol is CPA secure. The formal definition of this statement follows:

Definition 1. *Identity-based data aggregation protocol provides CPA security of smart meters if for all probabilistic polynomial-time (PPT) attackers $\mathcal{A}$ there exists a negligible function $negl(\cdot)$ such that*

$$Pr[ADV_{\mathcal{A}}^{CPAsecurity} = 1] = 1/2 + negl(\cdot).$$

Similarly, the **unlinkability game of smart meters** for identity-based data aggregation protocol is defined as follows:

1. The initialization and registration phases of identity-based data aggregation protocol is run, and the attacker gets the identity and other public parameters.
2. The attacker outputs two metering plaintexts m_0 and m_1 with the same length.
3. The challenger chooses a random bit $b \in \{0, 1\}$, and assigns m_b for the first honest smart meter and $m_{\bar{b}}$ for the second honest smart meter.
4. The remain parts of protocol are executed, and the attacker want to determine b.
5. Finally, the attacker outputs a guess bit b'. If $b = b'$, then it wins the game, and the output of this game is denoted as 1, and 0 otherwise.

If the attacker only has a negligible winning probability in the above game, then we say the identity-based data aggregation protocol is unlinkable. The formal definition of this statement follows:

Definition 2. *Identity-based data aggregation protocol provides unlinkability of smart meters if for all PPT attackers $\mathcal{A}$ there exists a negligible function $negl(\cdot)$ such that*

$$Pr[ADV_{\mathcal{A}}^{unlinkability} = 1] = 1/2 + negl(\cdot).$$

3   Wang et al.'s Identity-Based Data Aggregation Protocol

In this section, we review Wang et al.'s identity-based data aggregation protocol, which is consist of five phases.

(1) *Initialization Phase:* Private key generator (PKG) generates the bilinear group parameters $(G, G_T, e : G \times G \to G_T)$, where groups G and G_T have a prime order $p > 2^\iota$, where ι is a secure parameter. Let g be a generator of G and g_t be a generator of G_T. Then, PKG chooses $x \in_R Z_p$, sets $y = g^x$ and selects two cryptographic hash function $H : \{0, 1\}^* \to G$ and $H_2 : \{0, 1\}^* \to G$. Thus, the master public key of PKG is $mpk = (p, g, g_t, G, G_T, e, y, H, H_2)$ and the master secret key is $msk = x$.

(2) *Registration Phase:* Assuming that there are N smart meters in the collector's domain. Let ID_{ESP} be the identity of ESP, ID_c be the identity of collector and ID_i be the identity of ith smart grid device. When the ESP, the collector and the smart meters make registration to the system, the PKG generates the private keys $d_{ID_{ESP}} = H(ID_{ESP})^x$, $d_{ID_c} = H(ID_c)^x$ and $d_{ID_i} = H(ID_i)^x$ for the ESP, the collector, and the ith smart meter respectively. Finally, the PKG computes $W = e(H(ID_{ESP}), y)$, and sends it to all smart meters.

(3) *Collecting Phase*
   - **smart meter:** When the collector needs to collect the metering data m_i for the ith smart grid device, the smart meter chooses $r_i \in Z_p$ randomly and computes a ciphertext $CT_i = (c_{1i}, c_{2i}) = (g^{r_i}, g_t^{m_i} \cdot W^{r_i})$. We assume that collector collects the metering data from N smart meters in

its domain. Then, the smart meter randomly chooses $r_{si} \in Z_p$ as the random number in its signature. Let T_i be the current time stamp. Finally, the smart meter computes its signature $V_i = d_{ID_i} \cdot H_2(c_{2i}||T_i)^{r_{si}}$, and sends (CT_i, V_i, T_i) to the collector.

- **collector:** After receiving (CT_i, V_i, T_i) from the ith smart grid device, the collector verifies the ciphertext of metering data by checking

$$e(g, V_i) = e(y, H(ID_i))e(c_{1i}, H_2(c_{2i}||T_i)).$$

The collector can also aggregately verify all the signatures from N different smart meters. If $e(g, \prod_{i=1}^{n} V_i^{\varrho_i}) = e(y, \prod_{i=1}^{n} H(ID_i)^{\varrho_i}) \prod_{i=1}^{n} e(c_{1i}, H_2(c_{2i}||T_i)^{\varrho_i})$ holds, then the N signatures are all true.

(4) *Aggregation Phase:* After receiving all the ciphertexts and signatures from N smart meters, the collector needs to aggregate the total power usage data in its domain. After the batch verification of all the signatures, the collector computes the aggregated ciphertext as $CT = \prod_{i=1}^{n} CT_i = (C_1, C_2) = (\prod_{i=1}^{n} c_{1i}, \prod_{i=1}^{n} c_{2i})$ and chooses a random number $r_c \in Z_p$ to compute the signature $\sigma = (U, V) = (g^{r_c}, d_{ID_c} \cdot H_2(C_2||T_c)^{r_c})$, where T_c is the current time stamp of collector.

(5) *Decryption Phase:* When the ESP receives (CT, σ), it firstly verifies the ciphertext by checking

$$e(g, V) = e(y, H(ID_c))e(U, H_2(C_2||T_c)).$$

If the signature is true, then it computes $\bar{M} = C_2/e(d_{ID_{esp}}, C_1)$. Then, the ESP can compute the discrete log of $\bar{M}$ on the base of g_t to obtain the total power usage data M.

4   Security Analysis of Wang's Protocol

The security properties of the cryptographic primitives used in Wang's protocol have been proved formally. The task of security analysis in this section is to which set(s) of colluding adversaries can break the CPA security or unlinkability of the protocol. For Wang et al.'s protocol, five sets of colluding attackers should be considered. We assume that the communication channels between all the parties are secure and authenticated.

Colluding I: The collector and $N - 1$ smart meters collude, which means that all but one smart meter are dishonest. In this case, the collector and $N - 1$ corrupted smart meters try to get the plaintext of the only honest smart meter.

Colluding II: The ESP and $N - 1$ smart meters collude to get the plaintext of the only honest smart meter.

Colluding III: The ESP and the collector collude to get the plaintexts of any honest smart meters.[1]

---

[1] Note that if an attacker controls the ESP and the collector, then it does not need to control any dishonest smart meters, and can easily recover the plaintexts of any designated smart meters.

Colluding IV: There are at least two smart meters, SM_i and SM_j, where $1 \leq i \neq j \leq N$, are honest. In this case, given two ciphertexts CT_i and CT_j, the ESP and $N - 2$ smart meters collude to determine that these two ciphertexts are associated with which smart meters.

Colluding V: There are at least two smart meters are honest. Given two ciphertexts CT_i and CT_j, the ESP, the collector and $N - 2$ smart meters collude to determine that these two ciphertexts are linked with which smart meters.[2]

4.1   Security Analysis of Colluding I

When the collector and $N - 1$ smart meters collude, assume that the honest smart meter is SM_i ($i \in \{1, \cdots, N\}$), and the ESP is also honest. The idea of our proof for this case is not prove the protocol directly, but instead to construct a reduction that reduces the CPA security of protocol to the CPA security of the underlying identity-based encryption scheme. More precisely, the underlying CPA security of identity-based encryption scheme is formulated as an outer game in a reduction where an outer attacker $\mathbb{A}$ calls the attacker $\mathcal{A}$ of the protocol's CPA secure game as his subroutine by simulating as the role of challenger $\mathcal{C}$ for him. By doing this, $\mathbb{A}$ benefits from $\mathcal{A}$'s winning power to break the underlying CPA security of identity-based encryption scheme, i.e., winning the outer CPA game which plays with an outer challenger $\mathbb{C}$. Since $\mathcal{C} = \mathbb{A}$, there are only three parties ($\mathbb{C}, \mathbb{A}, \mathcal{A}$) involved in this proof.

Theorem 1. *If the identity-based encryption scheme used in protocol is CPA secure, then Wang et al.'s protocol provides smart meter's data CPA security against collector and $N - 1$ smart meters.*

Proof: First, we show the reduction how $\mathbb{A}$ calls $\mathcal{A}$ as his subroutine to succeed in CPA security game, and then prove that $\mathbb{A}$ has non-negligible advantage in case $\mathcal{A}$ has non-negligible advantage.

> Step 1: In the outer CPA game, $\mathbb{A}$ is given the identity ID_{ESP} and other public parameters from $\mathbb{C}$ which he passes to $\mathcal{A}$ in the initialization and registration phases of the inner security game.
>
> Step 2: In the inner CPA security game, $\mathcal{A}$ outputs two plaintexts m_0 and m_1, which have the same size, to $\mathcal{C} = \mathbb{A}$, who sends m_0 and m_1 to $\mathbb{C}$.
>
> Step 3: $\mathbb{C}$ chooses $B \in \{0,1\}$, assigns m_B for the only honest smart meter SM_i, and the encrypts the corresponding plaintext $CT_i = Enc_{ID_{ESP}}(m_B)$ and sends it to $\mathbb{A}$.
>
> Step 4: $\mathcal{A}$ and $\mathbb{A}$ run the collection phase with CT_i used by SM_i. There, the attacker can gets the ciphertext CT_i, since it controls the collector. $\mathbb{A}$ also runs the aggregation phase with $\mathcal{A}$.

---

[2] Note that an identity-based signature is used to protect the integrity of ciphertext in Wang's protocol, so if the collector joins the colluding set, then the attacker can easily determine that the submitted ciphertexts are associated with which smart meters.

Step 5: $\mathcal{A}$ outputs a bit b', then $\mathbb{A}$ outputs the same bit $B' = b'$. If $B = B'$, then $\mathbb{A}$ wins the CPA security game, and the output of this game is 1, and 0 otherwise.

Now we show that $\mathbb{A}$ wins exactly as $\mathcal{A}$ wins. Due to the definition of winning the CPA game and the choice of B' as b', $Pr[ADV_{\mathbb{A}}^{CPAsecurity} = 1] = Pr[B = B'] = Pr[B = b']$. Since $CT_i = Enc_{ID_{ESP}}(m_B)$, by comparison with step 3 of the protocol's CPA security game, $B = b$, thus $Pr[ADV_{\mathbb{A}}^{CPAsecurity} = 1] = Pr[b = b'] = Pr[ADV_{\mathbb{A}}^{CPAsecurity} = 1]$.

After reduction, $\mathcal{A}$ has the identity ID_{ESP}, the public parameters, all plaintexts/ciphertexts of $N-1$ dishonest smart meters, ciphertext of SM_i and the product of all ciphertexts. However, $\mathcal{A}$ does not know the private key $d_{ID_{ESP}}$, and the knowledge of ciphertext CT_i is of no use for it.   □

4.2   Security Analysis of Colluding II

In this case, the ESP and $N-1$ dishonest smart meters can collude to get the plaintext of the only one honest smart meter SM_i. To show the security violation, we can provide a code for a PPT attacker $\mathcal{A}$ who achieves non-negligible advantage. The proof is described formally as follows:

Step 1: During the registration phase, the attacker $\mathcal{A}$ controlling the ESP generates the private key $d_{ID_{ESP}}$ corresponding to the identity ID_{ESP}.

Step 2: $\mathcal{A}$ outputs two plaintexts m_0 and m_1 with the same length.

Step 3: The challenger $\mathcal{C}$ selects a bit $b \in \{0,1\}$, and encrypts the corresponding plaintext as $CT_i = Enc_{ID_{ESP}}(m_b)$ with SM_i.

Step 4: During the collection phase, the attacker $\mathcal{A}$ controlling $N-1$ dishonest smart meters receives all plaintexts $\{m_j | 1 \leq j \leq N, j \neq i\}$ except for SM_i. $\mathcal{A}$ also can get the product of encrypted metering data CT, since it controls the ESP.

Step 5: $\mathcal{A}$ as controlling the ESP can decrypt $Dec_{d_{ID_{ESP}}}(CT) = M$ by using the private key $d_{ID_{ESP}}$. Then, $\mathcal{A}$ computes $m_i = M - \sum_{j=1, j\neq i}^{N} m_j$, and set

$$b' = \begin{cases} 0 & if \quad m_i = m_0 \\ 1 & if \quad m_i = m_1 \end{cases}$$

$b = 0 \Leftrightarrow m_0$ is chosen by $\mathcal{C}$ in Step 3 $\Leftrightarrow$

$$CT = \prod_{j=1, j\neq i}^{N} Enc_{ID_{ESP}}(m_j) * Enc_{ID_{ESP}}(m_0)$$

$\Leftrightarrow b' = 0$. Due to the correctness of the identity-based encryption scheme, $\mathcal{A}$ always wins the game, i.e., $Pr[Adv_{\mathcal{A}}^{CPAsecurity} = 1] = 1$.

4.3   Security Analysis of Colluding III

In this case, the ESP and collector can collude to get the plaintexts of any designated smart meters. The security violation of any honest smart meters' data can be easily proven formally as follows.

Step 1: During the registration phase, the attacker $\mathcal{A}$ controlling the ESP generates the private key $d_{ID_{ESP}}$ with respect to the identity ID_{ESP}.

Step 2: $\mathcal{A}$ outputs two plaintexts m_0 and m_1 with the same length.

Step 3: The challenger $\mathcal{C}$ controlling all honest smart meters selects a bit $b \in \{0, 1\}$, and encrypts the corresponding plaintext as $CT_i = Enc_{ID_{ESP}}(m_b)$ for any one honest smart meter SM_i $(1 \le i \le N)$.

Step 4: $\mathcal{A}$ and $\mathcal{C}$ the collection phase, and $\mathcal{A}$ receives all ciphertexts from N smart meters. $\mathcal{A}$ also can get the product of encrypted metering data CT, since it controls the ESP.

Step 5: $\mathcal{A}$ as controlling the ESP can decrypt the challenge ciphertext $Dec_{d_{ID_{ESP}}}(CT_i) = m_i$ and set

$$b' = \begin{cases} 0 & if \quad m_i = m_0 \\ 1 & if \quad m_i = m_1 \end{cases}$$

$b = 0 \Leftrightarrow m_0$ is chosen by $\mathcal{C}$ in Step 3 $\Leftrightarrow CT_i = Enc_{ID_{ESP}}(m_0) \Leftrightarrow b' = 0$. Due to the correctness of the identity-based encryption scheme, $\mathcal{A}$ always wins the game, i.e., $Pr[Adv_{\mathcal{A}}^{CPAsecurity} = 1] = 1$.

4.4   Security Analysis of Colluding IV

In this case, the ESP and $N - 2$ smart meters collude to break the data unlinkability between two honest smart meters SM_i and SM_j, where $1 \le i, j \le N$. The following proof show information-theoretic security, i.e., given the obtained information during the protocol, the success probability of attacker must be exactly $1/2$.

Theorem 2. *Wang et al.'s protocol provides data unlinkability against the ESP and $N - 2$ smart meters.*

Proof:

Step 1: In the outer CPA game, $\mathbb{A}$ is given the identity ID_{ESP} and other public parameters from $\mathbb{C}$ which he passes to $\mathcal{A}$ in the initialization and registration phases of the inner unlinkability game.

Step 2: In the inner unlinkability game, $\mathcal{A}$ outputs two plaintexts m_0 and m_1 for the two honest smart meter SM_i and SM_j, which have the same size, to $\mathcal{C} = \mathbb{A}$, who sends m_0 and m_1 to $\mathbb{C}$.

Step 3: $\mathbb{C}$ chooses $B \in \{0, 1\}$, encrypts the corresponding two plaintexts $(CT_i^*, CT_j^*) = (Enc_{ID_{ESP}}(m_B), Enc_{ID_{ESP}}(m_{\bar{B}}))$ and sends it to $\mathbb{A}$. $\mathbb{A}$ then associate CT_i^* with SM_i, and CT_j^* with SM_j.

Step 4: $\mathcal{A}$ and $\mathbb{A}$ run the collection phase with CT_i^* used by SM_i and CT_j^* used by SM_j. There, the attacker $\mathcal{A}$ controlling $N-2$ dishonest smart meters receives all plaintexts $\{m_t | 1 \leq t \leq N, t \neq i,j\}$ except for SM_i and SM_j. $\mathcal{A}$ also can get the product of encrypted metering data CT, since it controls the ESP. Then, $\mathbb{A}$ runs the aggregation phase with $\mathcal{A}$.

Step 5: $\mathcal{A}$ outputs a bit b', then $\mathbb{A}$ outputs the same bit $B' = b'$. If $B = B'$, then $\mathbb{A}$ wins the CPA security game, and the output of this game is 1, and 0 otherwise.

In Step 4, $\mathbb{A}$ as challenger submits two ciphertexts (CT_i^*, CT_j^*) associated with two honest smart meters, while $\mathcal{A}$ submits $N-2$ encrypted plaintexts for its dishonest smart meters. Then, $\mathbb{A}$ multiplies all encrypted data and sends it to $\mathcal{A}$ who decrypts the aggregated value only learns the sum of metering data, i.e., $M = \sum_{t=1}^{N} m_t$. Thus, in Step 5, $\mathcal{A}$ can determine b' based on $M' = M - \sum_{t=1, t \neq i,j}^{N} m_t = m_0 + m_1$. So the success probability under the given information is: $Pr(b' = b|M') = \frac{Pr[b'=b,M']}{Pr[M']}$. Here, $Pr[b' = b, M'] = Pr[b' = 1, b = 1, M'] + Pr[b' = 0, b = 0, M']$. Obviously, due to the security of identity-based homomorphic encryption scheme, M' does not depend on the assignment of m_0 and m_0 on SM_i and SM_j (i.e.,b), and b' is also independent on b. b is a random bit, so $P(b) = 1/2$. Thus, $Pr[b' = b, M'] = Pr[b' = 1, b = 1, M'] + Pr[b' = 0, b = 0, M'] = 1/2c \cdot Pr[b' = 1, M'] + 1/2 \cdot Pr[b' = 0, M'] = 1/2Pr[M']$, and $Pr(b' = b|M') = \frac{Pr[b'=b,M']}{Pr[M']} = 1/2$.

$\square$

4.5   Security Analysis of Colluding V

In this case, the ESP, the collector and $N-2$ dishonest smart meters can collude to break the unlinkability game. To show the security violation, we can provide a code for a PPT attacker $\mathcal{A}$ who achieves non-negligible advantage. The proof is described formally as follows:

Step 1: During the registration phase, the attacker $\mathcal{A}$ controlling the ESP generates the private key $d_{ID_{ESP}}$ corresponding to the identity ID_{ESP}.

Step 2: $\mathcal{A}$ outputs two plaintexts m_0 and m_1 with the same length.

Step 3: The challenger $\mathcal{C}$ selects a bit $b \in \{0,1\}$, and encrypts the corresponding plaintext as $CT_i = Enc_{ID_{ESP}}(m_b)$ and $CT_j = Enc_{ID_{ESP}}(m_{\bar{b}})$. The challenger $\mathcal{C}$ assigns m_b to SM_i and $m_{\bar{b}}$ to SM_j.

Step 4: During the collection phase, the attacker $\mathcal{A}$ controlling collector receives two individual encrypted metering data CT_i and CT_j from SM_i and SM_j. $\mathcal{A}$ also can get the product of encrypted metering data CT, since it controls the ESP.

Step 5: $\mathcal{A}$ as controlling the ESP can decrypt CT_i by using the private key $d_{ID_{ESP}}$, and set

$$b' = \begin{cases} 0 & if \quad Dec_{d_{ID_{ESP}}}(CT_i) = m_0 \\ 1 & if \quad Dec_{d_{ID_{ESP}}}(CT_i) = m_1 \end{cases}$$

$b = 0 \Leftrightarrow m_0$ is assigned to SM_i by $\mathcal{C}$ in Step 3 $\Leftrightarrow$

$$Dec_{d_{ID_{ESP}}}(CT_i) = Dec_{d_{ID_{ESP}}}(Enc_{ID_{ESP}}(m_0)) = m_0$$

$\Leftrightarrow b' = 0$. Due to the correctness of the identity-based encryption scheme, $\mathcal{A}$ always wins the game, i.e., $Pr[ADV_{\mathcal{A}}^{unlinkability} = 1] = 1$.

5   Conclusions

Security and privacy are the most important concerns in the data aggregation protocols for smart grid. We provide formal definitions of CPA security and unlinkability for the smart meters' metering data. We also use this formal methodology to analysis Wang et al.'s identity-based data aggregation protocol against fives colluding attacks. From analysis, we find that this protocol can only resist two colluding attacks, and thus it is not very secure in practical. Our methodology also can be used to analyse other data aggregation protocols in smart grid. The CPA security game can test the data security of the smart meters in protocol, while the unlinkability game can check the privacy protection of the smart meters in protocol.

References

1. Fadlullah, Z.M., Fouda, M.M., Kato, N., Takeuchi, A., Iwasaki, N., Nozaki, Y.: Toward intelligent machine-to-machine communications in smart grid. IEEE Commun. Mag. **49**(4), 60–65 (2011)
2. Liang, H., Choi, B., Zhuang, W., Shen, X.: Towards optimal energy store-carry-and-deliver for PHEVs Via V2G system. In: Proceedings of the IEEE INFOCOM 2012, pp. 25–30 (2012)
3. Li, F., Luo, B., Liu, P.: Secure information aggregation for smart grids using homomorphic encryption. In: Proceedings of the 1st IEEE International Conference on Smart Grid Communications, pp. 327–332 (2010)
4. Fan, C.-I., Huang, S.-Y., Lai, Y.-L.: Privacy-enhanced data aggregation scheme against internal attackers in smart grid. IEEE Trans. Ind. Inform. **10**(1), 666–675 (2014)
5. Lu, R., Liang, X., Li, X., Lin, X., Shen, X.: EPPA: an efficient and privacy-preserving aggregation scheme for secure smart grid communications. IEEE Trans. Parallel Distrib. Syst. **23**(9), 1621–1631 (2012)
6. Wang, Z.: An identity-based data aggregation protocol for the smart grid. IEEE Trans. Ind. Inform. **13**(5), 2428–2435 (2017)
7. Engel, D.: Wavelet-based load profile representation for smart meter privacy. In: Proceedings of the IEEE PES Innovative Smart Grid Technologies, ISGT 2013, U.S.A., pp. 1–6 (2013)
8. Erkin, Z.: Private data aggregation with groups for smart grids in a dynamic setting using CRT. In: IEEE International Workshop on Information Forensics and Security, WIFS 2015, Italy, pp. 1–5 (2015)
9. Erkin, Z., Tsudik, G.: Private computation of spatial and temporal power consumption with smart meters. In: Bao, F., Samarati, P., Zhou, J. (eds.) ACNS 2012. LNCS, vol. 7341, pp. 561–577. Springer, Heidelberg (2012). https://doi.org/10.1007/978-3-642-31284-7_33

10. Marmol, F.G., Sorge, C., Petrlic, R., Ugus, O., Westhoff, D., Perez, G.M.: Privacy-enhanced architecture for smart metering. Int. J. Inf. Secur. **12**(2), 67–82 (2013)
11. Castelluccia, C., Chan, A.C., Mykletun, E., Tsudik, G.: Efficient and provably secure aggregation of encrypted data in wireless sensor networks. ACM Trans. Sens. Netw. (TOSN) **5**(3), 20 (2009)
12. Bohli, J.-M., Sorge, C., Ugus, O.: A privacy model for smart metering. In: 2010 IEEE International Conference on Communications Workshops, ICC, pp. 1–5 (2010)
13. Katz, J., Lindell, Y.: Introduction to Modern Cryptography, 1st edn. CRC Press, Boca Raton (2007)

A More Efficient Secure Fully Verifiable Delegation Scheme for Simultaneous Group Exponentiations

Stephan Moritz and Osmanbey Uzunkol[(✉)]

Faculty of Mathematics and Computer Science, FernUniversität in Hagen,
Hagen, Germany
stephan.moritz@web.de, osmanbey.uzunkol@gmail.com

Abstract. Along with the recent advancements in cloud and mobile computing, secure and verifiable delegation of expensive computations to powerful servers has become a highly expedient and increasingly popular option. Group exponentiations (**GE**s) form one of the most expensive, though unavoidable, operations in order to utilize various security protocols since they are typically required as building blocks of advanced cryptographic technologies. In this paper, we address the problem of efficient, secure and verifiable delegation of simultaneous **GE**s. Firstly, we propose a secure, efficient and *fully verifiable* simultaneous delegation scheme InvDel using two servers one of which is assumed to be malicious. InvDel removes the requirement of computations of group inversions (**GI**s) completely while providing full verifiability. InvDel considerably improves the computational efficiency of the delegation, and it is the most efficient delegation scheme for **GE**s. To the best of our knowledge, InvDel is also the first secure delegation scheme for simultaneous **GE**s achieving full verifiability efficiently. Secondly, we give implementation results of InvDel in an Android application together with a comprehensive efficiency analysis with the previous results. For example, when the required CPU costs for a single **GE** are compared with a 3072-bit modulus, InvDel is at least 189-times (resp. 3-times) more efficient than the utilization of a local computation (resp. the utilization of the only available fully verifiable scheme introduced before). Furthermore, if the security level, whence the corresponding bit length, increases, then the advantage of InvDel becomes much more better if compared with the previous delegation schemes. Finally, we also utilize InvDel to speed-up the verification step of Schnorr's signatures.

Keywords: Verifiable and secure delegation
Cloud security and privacy · Applied cryptography
Lightweight cryptography for mobile security

1   Introduction

With the recent advancements in cloud computing and the widespread proliferation of mobile devices like smart phones, RFID tags, or cheap sensor nodes,

© Springer Nature Switzerland AG 2018
I. Traore et al. (Eds.): ISDDC 2018, LNCS 11317, pp. 74–93, 2018.
https://doi.org/10.1007/978-3-030-03712-3_7

delegating (or outsourcing) expensive computations from week devices to more powerful cloud server providers (CSPs) has gained lots of attention and become very attractive since it offers particularly energy-efficient and cost-effective solutions for mobile resource-constrained devices. The main reason is that most costly operations could otherwise be very difficult to perform locally for such resource-constrained devices in most real-life applications (if not totally unrealizable). However, with the delegation of a computational task to CSPs, users not only reveal their (potentially) sensitive data to *untrusted* CSPs, but lose unfortunately also completely their control over the delegated data. Protecting sensitive data from potentially malicious CSPs effectively while assuring at the same time the correctness of the delegated computation efficiently requires new lightweight privacy- and anonymity-oriented security protocols. However, many security protocols are typically resource-consuming because of the underlying heavy arithmetical operations. In contrast to general purpose cryptographic techniques like garbled circuits [20] and fully homomorphic encryption [9], delegation of those expensive *cryptographic* operations has become an increasingly popular and more efficient way to be able to design delegetable privacy- and anonymity-oriented security protocols [4,6,7,10,21]. Beside the security requirements, ensuring desired level of verifiability of the correctness of the delegated cryptographic operations is a highly indispensable requirement in many application scenarios of security protocols (e.g. applications requiring verifications of digital signatures and other advanced authentication techniques) [11,15].

Among all the cryptographic primitives, *group exponentiations* (**GE**s) form one of the most expensive operations which are predominantly used in many advanced cryptographic protocols; hence they form highly expensive but indispensable building blocks of most advanced security technologies. For cryptographic purposes, the groups are usually required to be chosen as follows:

- A cyclic group $\mathbb{G}$ of large prime order q (the *discrete logarithm setting*). Examples are *either* a subgroup of the multiplicative group modulo a prime number p of order q (i.e. q is a divisor of $p - 1$), *or* a cyclic subgroup of an elliptic curve E over a prime field $\mathbb{F}_p$ of order q.
- The multiplicative group modulo a large RSA-modulus $n = pq$, where p and q are large distinct primes.

In this paper, we concentrate our attention on the delegation of **GE**s in cryptographically suitable cyclic groups (hence the discrete logarithm setting) following many previous delegation schemes in the literature.

Related Work. Chaum and Pedersen [5] introduced the concept of wallets with observers, which allows a third party service to install an untrusted hardware component on a user's device that helps the user to compute cryptographic operations including **GE**s. Hohenberger and Lysyanskaya [10] subsequently formalized the notion of secure and verifiable delegation of **GE**s by introducing a simulation-based security model in the presence of malicious powerful helpers, which we simply call *servers* throughout this paper. Hohenberger and Lysyanskaya [10], and later Chen *et al.* [6] proposed secure delegation schemes with verifiability probabilities $1/2$ and $2/3$, respectively, by using two servers at most one of which is assumed to be malicious (which they abbreviate as the *OMTUP-model*). The first delegation scheme for **GE**s using a single untrusted server is introduced by Wang *et al.* [19] with a verifiability probability $1/2$. There is also another scheme of Cavallo *et al.* [4] with a verifiability probability $1/2$ by using a single server offering also a secure delegation scheme for **GI**s. However, it is shown recently by Chevalier *et al.* [7] that the scheme in [19] has severe security and privacy issues which cannot be fixed effectively. Furthermore, the results in [7] imply that a secure *non-interactive* delegation scheme with a single untrusted server requires an online computation of a **GE** even without any verifiability guarantees. Kiraz and Uzunkol [11] introduced the first two-round secure delegation scheme using a single malicious server with a variable verifiability probability depending on a prescribed constant small integer c. In particular, the scheme in [11] is the first one having an adjustable verification probability; the larger the value c is, the better the verifiability probability is (at the expense of more group multiplications). However, the communication overhead of the scheme in [11] is relatively high. In particular, none of these schemes achieve strong verification property (*full verifiability*, i.e. with a verifiability probability 1), and they require online computations (sometimes a large number) of **GI**s. Recently, Ren *et al.* [15] proposed the *first* two-round fully verifiable secure delegation scheme for **GE**s under the OMTUP-model at the expense of online computations of five **GI**s.

Both Kuppusamy and Rangasamy [12] and Zhou *et al.* [21] introduced *special* purpose secure delegation schemes for modular exponentiations (**ME**s) by hiding some prime moduli via Chinese Remainder Theorem (CRT), where the group is chosen to be a subgroup of the multiplicative group modulo p. The reason of hiding some prime moduli is to obtain *non-interactive*, i.e. single round, secure delegation schemes. Very recently, Uzunkol *et al.* [18] propose a highly efficient non-interactive delegation scheme for modular exponentiations using the same strategy (i.e. by hiding the prime modulus via CRT). However, hiding a prime modulus has restricted application areas as it is typically the case that the prime number p is part of the public information of the security protocols; hence it is rather difficult in practice to keep it secret. Furthermore, it is shown in [18] that [12] offers no verifiability. Moreover, we notice that [21] does not provide the desired security guarantees.

Advanced security protocols usually require n-simultaneous multiplications of **GE**s (also called sometimes batch **GE**s), where $n \geq 1$ is the number of simultaneous **GE**s. Several papers introduced secure delegation schemes for simultaneous **GE**s (see [6,15] for schemes in the OMTUP-model and [11] for a scheme with a single untrusted server), which reduce the computational and communication overhead of the delegation when compared with delegating each **GE** individually and multiplying the outputs subsequently. However, none of these schemes achieve the challenging full verifiability property; even worse it is shown in [18] that the scheme in [15] offers much less verifiability probability (i.e. only

$\approx 1/2$ if n tends to infinity) instead of the original almost full verifiability claim (i.e. ≈ 1 if n tends to infinity).

Our Contribution. In this paper, we introduce a secure, efficient and fully verifiable delegation n-simultaneous scheme InvDel for any positive integer $n \geq 1$ with the following properties:

1. InvDel is the most efficient secure delegation scheme when compared with the previous schemes requiring no computation of **GI**s by the delegator. For example, InvDel (with $n = 1$) requires only 21 group multiplications, thence computationally more than 24 times more efficient than the fully verifiable scheme of Ren *et al.* [15].
2. InvDel is the *first* fully verifiable secure delegation scheme for n-simultaneous **GE**s. Compared with delegating each **GE** individually, InvDel requires computation of much less group multiplications; it only needs $13n + 8$ group multiplications instead of $21n$ group multiplications (required in the case of individual delegations of n different **GE**s).
3. We implement InvDel in an Android application and give a comparative efficiency analysis with the previous schemes to illustrate the computational efficiency via the utilization of InvDel in a mobile device. Furthermore, InvDel is implemented in various security levels to show the fact that the delegator benefits much more if the bit size of the prime modulus increases when compared with the previous schemes or computing **GE**s locally.
4. We utilize InvDel as a subroutine to obtain an efficient and delegation-secure verification step of Schnorr's signatures.

We describe InvDel for simplicity only in the case that $\mathbb{G}$ is a subgroup of the multiplicative group modulo a prime number p of prime order q throughout the paper. However, InvDel can also be effectively utilized to delegate scalar multiplications of a cyclic subgroup of an elliptic curve. Hence, InvDel provides a *generic* fully verifiable secure simultaneous delegation scheme for any cyclic group of prime order which are used in current security protocols in contrast to [12,18].

Road Map. The rest of the paper is organized as follows: Sect. 2 deals with the definitions and a security model for secure and verifiable delegation of **GE**s. In Sect. 3, we introduce our scheme InvDel and give its detailed security analysis. Subsequently, comparison and implementation results are given in Sect. 4. We apply InvDel to introduce a delegation-secure verification step for Schnorr's signatures in Sect. 5. Then, Sect. 6 concludes the paper.

2 Preliminaries and Security Model

This section starts with the basic notation and terminology. We revisit the simulation-based security notions of Hohenberger and Lyanskaya [10] which we later require to give the security analysis of InvDel in Sect. 3. This section ends with the main steps of a secure delegation scheme for **GE**s.

2.1 Basic Notation and Terminology

We denote by $\mathbb{Z}_m$ the quotient ring $\mathbb{Z}/m\mathbb{Z}$ for a natural number $m \in \mathbb{N}^{>1}$. Similarly, $\mathbb{Z}_m^*$ denotes the multiplicative group of $\mathbb{Z}_m$. Let $\sigma \in 1^\lambda$ be a global security parameter. We assume that there exists an algorithm GroupGen which takes σ as its input, and outputs a prime number p, the description of a cyclic subgroup $\mathbb{G}$ of $\mathbb{Z}_p^*$, its prime order q, and a fixed generator g of $\mathbb{G}$ [1]. The process of running a (*probabilistic*) algorithm Alg, which accepts $x_1, x_2, \ldots$ as inputs, and produces an output y, is denoted by $y \leftarrow \mathsf{Alg}(x_1, x_2, \ldots)$. Let $(z_{\mathsf{Alg}_1}, z_{\mathsf{Alg}_2}) \leftarrow (\mathsf{Alg}_1(x_1, x_2, \ldots), \mathsf{Alg}_2(y_1, y_2, \ldots))$ denote the process of running an *interactive* protocol between two algorithms Alg_1 and Alg_2 such that $x_1, x_2, \ldots$ are inputs of Alg_1, $y_1, y_2, \ldots$ are inputs of Alg_2 (possibly with further random coins), and z_{Alg_1} and z_{Alg_2} are the outputs, respectively. The expression $x \leftarrow a$ also denotes assigning the value of a to a variable x as usual.

2.2 Security Assumptions and Model

We follow exactly the lines of [10] for the security definitions and the model of the delegated cryptographic computation:

We assume that a delegation scheme consists of two types of parties called as the client $\mathcal{C}$ (*trusted* but potentially resource-constrained part) and servers (*untrusted* but powerful part) $\mathcal{U}$, where $\mathcal{U}$ can again consist of one or more parties. $(\mathcal{C}, \mathcal{U})$ denotes a delegated-secure implementation of a cryptographic algorithm Alg if $\mathcal{C}$ and $\mathcal{U}$ jointly implements $\mathsf{Alg} = \mathcal{C}^{\mathcal{U}}$, and $\mathcal{C}$ is given oracle access to a malicious adversarial software $\mathcal{U}'$ in place of $\mathcal{U}$, i.e. $\mathcal{U} \neq \mathcal{U}'$, such that $\mathcal{U}'$ cannot obtain any information about both the input and the output of $\mathcal{C}^{\mathcal{U}'}$ although acting maliciously every time it is invoked by means of recording its own computation over time. Furthermore, there exists also an adversarial environment $\mathcal{E}$ generating adversarial inputs to Alg. Therefore, the adversary $\mathcal{A}$ is modeled in [10] by a pair of two algorithms $\mathcal{A} = (\mathcal{E}, \mathcal{U}')$. The *fundamental assumption* is that $\mathcal{E}$ and $\mathcal{U}'$ can only develop a joint strategy together until interacting with the delegator $\mathcal{C}$, but they will not have a direct communication thereafter [10]. According to this assumption, the inputs of Alg can be classified into the following subcategories:

- *honest, secret* inputs *only* available to $\mathcal{C}$,
- *honest, protected* inputs available to both $\mathcal{C}$ and $\mathcal{E}$ but not available to $\mathcal{U}'$,
- *honest, unprotected* inputs available to $\mathcal{C}$, $\mathcal{E}$, and $\mathcal{U}'$,
- *adversarial, protected* inputs available to $\mathcal{C}$, $\mathcal{E}$, but not available to $\mathcal{U}'$,
- *adversarial, unprotected* inputs available to $\mathcal{C}$, $\mathcal{E}$, and $\mathcal{U}'$.

---

[1] As we outlined in Sect. 1, we here only concentrate on the prime order subgroups of $\mathbb{Z}_p^*$ as in the previous schemes. However, the results are general, thence can be generalized easily to an arbitrary cyclic group $\mathbb{G}$ of prime order q that is used in cryptographic protocols.

Definition 1 [10] *(Delegated Security).*
Let $\mathsf{Alg}(\cdot,\cdot,\cdot,\cdot,\cdot)$ be an algorithm (with five inputs). A pair of algorithms $(\mathcal{C},\mathcal{U})$ is said to be a delegated-secure implementation of Alg if the following properties hold:

Completeness. $\mathcal{C}^{\mathcal{U}}$ is a correct implementation of Alg.

Security. For all probabilistic polynomial-time adversaries (PPT adversaries) $\mathcal{A} = (\mathcal{E},\mathcal{U}')$, there exist probabilistic expected polynomial-time simulators $(\mathcal{S}_1,\mathcal{S}_2)$ such that the following pairs of random variables are computationally indistinguishable. We assume that the honestly-generated inputs are chosen by a process $\mathcal{I}$.

- **Pair One:** $EVIEW_{real} \sim EVIEW_{ideal}$ *(The external adversary $\mathcal{E}$ learns nothing)*
- **Pair Two:** $UVIEW_{real} \sim UVIEW_{ideal}$: *(The untrusted software $\mathcal{E}$ learns nothing)*

The details of the experiments **Pair One** and **Pair Two** can be found in [10, pp. 269–271] which we require in our security analysis.

The OMTUP-Model. Hohenberger and Lyanskaya [10] presented one malicious version of *two-untrusted programs* (OMTUP-model) as we discussed in Sect. 1. In the OMTUP-model, we have two servers $\mathcal{U}_1$ and $\mathcal{U}_2$, i.e. the adversary is given by $\mathcal{A} = (\mathcal{E},\mathcal{U}_1,\mathcal{U}_2)$. The adversarial environment $\mathcal{E}$ writes the code for two different programs $\mathcal{U}' = (\mathcal{U}_1',\mathcal{U}_2')$ and gives them to $\mathcal{C}$. Afterwards, the communication between any two of $\mathcal{E}$, $\mathcal{U}_1'$ and $\mathcal{U}_2'$ must solely pass through $\mathcal{C}$. We further assume that only one of the two programs $\mathcal{U}_1'$ and $\mathcal{U}_2'$ can act maliciously. We now give the definitions of efficiency and verifiability under the OMTUP-model.

Definition 2 *(α-Efficiency).*
A pair of algorithms $(\mathcal{C},\mathcal{U}_1,\mathcal{U}_2)$ are called an α-efficient delegated-implementation of Alg if

1. $\mathcal{C}^{(\mathcal{U}_1,\mathcal{U}_2)}$ is a complete implementation of Alg, and
2. For all inputs x, the running time of $\mathcal{C}$ is smaller than an α-multiplicative factor of the running time of $\mathsf{Alg}(x)$.

Definition 3 *(β-Verifiability).*
A pair of algorithms $(\mathcal{C},\mathcal{U}_1,\mathcal{U}_2)$ are called a β-verifiable delegated implementation of Alg if

1. $\mathcal{C}^{(\mathcal{U}_1,\mathcal{U}_2)}$ is a complete implementation of Alg, and
2. For all inputs x, if either $\mathcal{U}_1'$ or $\mathcal{U}_2'$ deviates from its advertised functionality during the execution of $\mathcal{C}^{(\mathcal{U}_1,\mathcal{U}_2)}(x)$, $\mathcal{C}$ will detect the error with probability larger than β. In particular, if $\mathcal{C}$ will always detect the error, except with a negligible probability, i.e. $1 - β$ is negligibly small, then a pair of algorithms $(\mathcal{C},\mathcal{U}_1,\mathcal{U}_2)$ are called a fully verifiable delegated implementation of Alg.

Definition 4 (α, β-*Delegated Secure Implementation*).
A pair of algorithms $(\mathcal{C}, \mathcal{U}_1, \mathcal{U}_2)$ are called an (α, β)-delegated secure implementation of Alg if they are both α-efficient and β-verifiable. In particular, a pair of algorithms $(\mathcal{C}, \mathcal{U}_1, \mathcal{U}_2)$ are called a fully verifiable $(\alpha, 1)$-delegated secure implementation of an algorithm Alg if they are both α-efficient and a fully verifiable delegated implementation of Alg.

2.3   Steps of the Delegation of Group Exponentiations

In order to securely delegate the computation of n-simultaneous **GE**s of the form $u_1^{a_1} \cdots u_n^{a_n}$ (with the base elements $u_1, \cdots, u_n \in \mathbb{G}$, the exponents $a_1, \cdots, a_n \in \mathbb{Z}_p^*$, and $n \in \mathbb{Z}^{\geq 1}$), a delegation scheme requires a *precomputation step*, which we call the Rand scheme. Rand produces some pseudorandom pairs $(k, g^k) \in \mathbb{Z}_p \times \mathbb{G}$ in order to randomize the elements u_i and a_i before delegating the **GE**s to the servers $\mathcal{U}_1$ and $\mathcal{U}_2$ for $1 \leq i \leq n$. One possibility of implementing Rand is to perform the computation of the pairs (k, g^k) offline if $\mathcal{C}$ is able to compute **GE**s alone, or there exists a trusted server computing the pairs (k, g^k) on behalf of $\mathcal{C}$ using some speed-up techniques [1,8,14,16], which later be loaded to $\mathcal{C}$.

If $\mathcal{C}$ is incapable of computing **GE**s and there exists no *online* trusted server computing **GE**s on behalf of $\mathcal{C}$, then usually a preprocessing technique (see [2,3,19]) is used to implement Rand. Such a preprocessing technique starts with a fixed number of pairs $(x_i, g^{x_i}) \in \mathbb{Z}_p^* \times \mathbb{G}$, say $1 \leq i \leq t$, the so-called *static table*, which could be computed *only once* either by $\mathcal{C}$ itself or by an *offline* trusted server at the initialization of the delegation scheme. Then, a *dynamic table* is constructed by using the static table yielding to new pairs (dynamic table) which have distribution statistically close to the uniform distribution. The security of these preprocessing schemes are based on the subset sum problem [2,3,19].

Using the pairs (k, g^k) from Rand, the base elements $u_1, \cdots, u_n$ and the exponents $a_1, \cdots, a_n$ are subsequently randomized before delegating the computation of $u_1^{a_1} \cdots u_n^{a_n}$. Note that we denote throughout the paper by $\mathcal{U}_i(x, h)$ the delegation of the computation h^x with $(x, h) \in \mathbb{Z}_p^* \times \mathbb{G}$ for $i = 1, 2$. Similarly, $\mathcal{U}_i(\cdot^{-1}, \alpha)$ denotes the delegation of the computation of α^{-1} for $\alpha \in \mathbb{Z}_p^*$ for $i = 1, 2$. After receiving the queries from $\mathcal{U}_1$ and $\mathcal{U}_2$, the results are de-randomized and the output values are verified (possibly by using carefully chosen pairs from Rand).

3   InvDel: A Secure and Fully Verifiable Group Simultaneous Exponentiation Scheme

In this section, we propose a new secure simultaneous delegation scheme InvDel for group exponentiations and give its security analysis under the OMTUP-model. In particular, InvDel adapts and improves some recent ideas of [4,17] to the delegation of **GE**s by completely removing the requirement of the computation of **GI**s by $\mathcal{C}$ while providing full verifiability for simultaneous delegations of **GE**s.

Let p be a prime number and $\mathbb{G}$ be a cyclic subgroup of $\mathbb{Z}_p^*$ of prime order q. Our aim is to delegate the computation of $u_1^{a_1} \cdot u_2^{a_2} \cdots u_n^{a_n}$, where $n \in \mathbb{Z}^{\geq 1}$, $u_i \in \mathbb{G}$, and $a_i \in \mathbb{Z}_q^*$ for $1 \leq i \leq n$. In particular, InvDel is introduced in a generalized form (corresponding exactly to a classical single delegation scheme for the computation u^a with $u \in \mathbb{G}$ and $a \in \mathbb{Z}_q^*$ by letting $n = 1$).

3.1 Our Scheme

Let $\mathcal{C}$ be the trusted component and $\mathcal{U}_1$, $\mathcal{U}_2$ be potentially untrusted servers in the OMTUP-model. The description of InvDel is as follows:

Public parameters. $n \in \mathbb{Z}^{\geq 1}$, prime numbers p and q, description of a subgroup $\mathbb{G}$ of $\mathbb{Z}_p^*$ of order q, a fixed generator g of $\mathbb{G}$ (obtained by running the algorithm GroupGen with the input σ as outlined in Sect. 2).

Private parameters. The bases $u_1, \cdots, u_n \in \mathbb{G}$ and the exponents $a_1, \cdots, a_n \in \mathbb{Z}_q^*$.

Precomputation. Using Rand (as described in Sect. 2), $\mathcal{C}$ first outputs for $1 \leq i \leq n$

$$(t_1, g^{t_1}), \cdots, (t_n, g^{t_n}) \in \mathbb{Z}_q^* \times \mathbb{G},$$

and

$$(\ell, g^\ell), (r_1, g^{r_1}), (r_2, g^{r_2}), (\alpha, g^\alpha), (\beta, g^\beta) \in \mathbb{Z}_q^* \times \mathbb{G}.$$

Then, $\mathcal{C}$ sets $R_1 := g^{r_1}$, $R_2 := g^{r_2}$, $v := g^\alpha$, and $\mu := g^\beta$.

Masking. The base elements u_i are randomized by $\mathcal{C}$ with

$$w_i = u_i \cdot v, \ 1 \leq i \leq n. \tag{1}$$

Then, we have

$$
\begin{aligned}
u_1^{a_1} \cdots u_n^{a_n} &= w_1^{a_1} \cdots w_n^{a_n} \cdot v^{-(\sum_{i=1}^n a_i)} \\
&= w_1^{a_1} \cdots w_n^{a_n} \cdot g^{-\alpha(\sum_{i=1}^n a_i)} \\
&= w_1^{a_1} \cdots w_n^{a_n} \cdot g^{-\alpha(\sum_{i=1}^n a_i) - \beta} \cdot g^\beta \\
&= w_1^{a_1} \cdots w_n^{a_n} \cdot g^\gamma \cdot \mu,
\end{aligned}
$$

where $\gamma := -\alpha \cdot (a_1 + \cdots + a_n) - \beta$.

First Queries to $\mathcal{U}_1$. $\mathcal{C}$ chooses $c_1, c_2, c_3 \in \mathbb{Z}_q^*$ randomly, and sends the following queries in random order to $\mathcal{U}_1$:

1. $\mathcal{U}_1(-r_1 \cdot t_i^{-1}, w_i \cdot g^{t_i}) \longleftarrow D_{11i} = w_i^{-r_1/t_i} g^{-r_1}$
   for $1 \leq i \leq n$,

2. $\mathcal{U}_1(\cdot^{-1}, c_1 \cdot r_1) \longleftarrow D_{12} = c_1^{-1} \cdot r_1^{-1}$,
3. $\mathcal{U}_1(\cdot^{-1}, c_2 \cdot r_2) \longleftarrow D_{13} = c_2^{-1} \cdot r_2^{-1}$,
4. $\mathcal{U}_1(\cdot^{-1}, c_3 \cdot \ell) \longleftarrow D_{14} = c_3^{-1} \cdot \ell^{-1}$.

First Queries to $\mathcal{U}_2$. Similarly, $\mathcal{C}$ sends the following queries in random order to $\mathcal{U}_2$:

1. $\mathcal{U}_2(-r_2 \cdot t_i^{-1}, w_i g^{t_i}) \longleftarrow D_{21i} = w_i^{-r_2/t_i} g^{-r_2}$
   for $1 \le i \le n$,
2. $\mathcal{U}_2(\cdot^{-1}, c_1 r_1) \longleftarrow D_{22} = c_1^{-1} \cdot r_1^{-1}$,
3. $\mathcal{U}_2(\cdot^{-1}, c_2 r_2) \longleftarrow D_{23} = c_2^{-1} \cdot r_2^{-1}$,
4. $\mathcal{U}_2(\cdot^{-1}, c_3 \ell) \longleftarrow D_{24} = c_3^{-1} \cdot \ell^{-1}$.

First Verification of the Correctness of the Outputs of $\{\mathcal{U}_1, \mathcal{U}_2\}$. Upon receiving the queries D_{11i}, D_{1j} from $\mathcal{U}_1$ and D_{21i}, D_{2j} from $\mathcal{U}_2$, $1 \le i \le n$, $2 \le j \le 4$, $\mathcal{C}$ verifies

$$D_{12} \overset{?}{=} D_{22}, \ D_{13} \overset{?}{=} D_{23}, \ D_{14} \overset{?}{=} D_{24}. \tag{2}$$

If Eq. (2) hold simultaneously, then $\mathcal{C}$ computes

$$w_i^{-r_1/t_i} = D_{11i} \cdot R_1, \ w_i^{-r_2/t_i} = D_{21i} \cdot R_2, \ 1 \le i \le n. \tag{3}$$

Furthermore, $\mathcal{C}$ computes

$$r_1^{-1} = c_1 \cdot D_{12}, \ r_2^{-1} = c_2 \cdot D_{13}, \ \ell^{-1} = c_3 \cdot D_{14}, \tag{4}$$

and sets for $1 \le i \le n$

$$s_{1i} := -a_i \cdot t_i \cdot r_1^{-1}, \ s_{2i} := -a_i t_i \cdot r_2^{-1}. \tag{5}$$

If the verification step fails, then $\mathcal{C}$ outputs $\perp$.

Second Queries to $\mathcal{U}_1$. $\mathcal{C}$ sends the following queries in random order to $\mathcal{U}_1$:

1. $\mathcal{U}_1(\gamma \cdot \ell^{-1}, g^\ell) \longleftarrow D_{15} = g^\gamma$,
2. $\mathcal{U}_1(s_{2i}, w_i^{-r_2/t_i}) \longleftarrow D_{16i} = (w_i^{-r_2/t_i})^{s_{2i}}$
   for $1 \le i \le n$.

Second Queries to $\mathcal{U}_2$. $\mathcal{C}$ sends the following queries in random order to $\mathcal{U}_2$:

1. $\mathcal{U}_2(\gamma \ell^{-1}, g^\ell) \longleftarrow D_{25} = g^\gamma$,
2. $\mathcal{U}_2(s_{1i}, w_i^{-r_1/t_i}) \longleftarrow D_{26i} = (w_i^{-r_1/t_i})^{s_{1i}}$
   for $1 \le i \le n$.

Second Verification of the Correctness of the Outputs of $\{\mathcal{U}_1, \mathcal{U}_2\}$.
Upon receiving the queries D_{15} and D_{16i} from $\mathcal{U}_1$, and D_{25} and D_{26i} from $\mathcal{U}_2$, $1 \leq i \leq n$, respectively, $\mathcal{C}$ verifies

$$D_{15} \stackrel{?}{=} D_{25}, \; D_{16i} \stackrel{?}{=} D_{26i}, \; 1 \leq i \leq n. \tag{6}$$

Recovering $u_1^{a_1} \cdots u_n^{a_n}$. If Eq. (6) hold simultaneously, then $\mathcal{C}$ computes

$$u_1^{a_1} \cdots u_n^{a_n} = D_{15} \cdot D_{161} \cdots D_{16n} \cdot \mu. \tag{7}$$

If the verification step fails, then $\mathcal{C}$ outputs $\perp$.

Remark 1. Inspired by a recent scheme in [17], InvDel improves the secure delegation scheme of **GI**s first proposed in [4] using a single server.

3.2   Removing the Computation of Modular Inversions

Although modular inversions (**MI**s) of the form t_i, $1 \leq i \leq n$, need to be computed in InvDel, these computations are completely independent of the simultaneous delegation of $u_1^{a_1} \cdot u_2^{a_2} \cdots u_n^{a_n}$. Therefore, it is also possible to delegate the computations of **GI**s. At the set up phase, values of the form (t_i, t_i^{-1}, g^{t_i}), $1 \leq i \leq n$, can be computed *only once*. Afterwards, at each delegation of $u_1^{a_1} \cdots u_n^{a_n}$, new couples (ℓ_i, g^{ℓ_i}) can be generated, and the computation of ℓ_i^{-1}, $1 \leq i \leq n$, can easily be delegated for later use.

In particular, InvDel can be extended to delegate the computations of **GI**s by choosing random elements $c_i' \in \mathbb{Z}_q^*$, $1 \leq i \leq n$, and adding queries for $\mathcal{U}_1$:

$$- \mathcal{U}_1(\cdot^{-1}, c_i' \cdot \ell_i) \longleftarrow D_{17i} = c_i'^{-1} \cdot \ell_i^{-1}, \; 1 \leq i \leq n,$$

and queries for $\mathcal{U}_2$:

$$- \mathcal{U}_2(\cdot^{-1}, c_i' \cdot \ell_i) \longleftarrow D_{27i} = c_i'^{-1} \cdot \ell_i^{-1}, \; 1 \leq i \leq n,$$

comparing $D_{17i} \stackrel{?}{=} D_{27i}$, and finally computing $c_i' \cdot D_{17i}$. These new steps lead to securely delegate ℓ_i^{-1} by only a single query for each server (i.e. in the second round of InvDel) and 2 modular multiplications (**MM**s)) in $\mathbb{Z}_q^*$ for each $1 \leq i \leq n$. Hence, by doing so InvDel requires neither online nor offline computation of **GI**s provided that elements (t_i, t_i^{-1}, g^{t_i}) are stored *only once* at the initialization of InvDel. In particular for $n = 1$, InvDel requires only 2 **MM**s in $\mathbb{Z}_q^*$ to delegate the computation of a single **MI**, whose local computation by $\mathcal{C}$ would otherwise correspond to approximately 100 **MM**s [11].

3.3   Security and Efficiency Analysis

We now give a security analysis of InvDel based on the security model introduced in [10].

Theorem 1. *In the OMTUP-model, the algorithms* $(\mathcal{C}, \mathcal{U}_1, \mathcal{U}_2)$ *are a* $(\mathcal{O}(1/\log q), 1)$*-delegated secure implementations of* InvDel, *where the inputs* $((a_1, a_2, \cdots, a_n), (u_1, u_2, \cdots, u_n)) \in (\mathbb{Z}_q^*)^n \times \mathbb{G}^n$ *may be honest, secret; or honest, protected; or adversarial, protected.*

Proof. We start with the completeness of InvDel:

Completeness. Suppose that both $\mathcal{U}_1$ and $\mathcal{U}_2$ execute InvDel honestly. It is straightforward to see for $j = 2, 3, 4$ that we have $D_{1j} = D_{2j}$. Hence, the first verification step of InvDel is complete. Now we have for each $j = 2, 3, 4$ and for each $1 \le i \le n$ the equalities

$$c_{j-1} \cdot D_{1i} = c_{j-1} \cdot c_{j-1}^{-1} r_{j-1}^{-1},$$

$$D_{11i} \cdot R_1 = w_i^{-r_1/t_i} g^{-r_1} \cdot g^{r_1} = w_i^{-r_1/t_i}, D_{21i} \cdot R_2 = w_i^{-r_2/t_i}.$$

Then, the second verification is also complete since we have $D_{15} = D_{25}$ by the first verification step and the following equalities hold for each $1 \le i \le n$:

$$\begin{aligned}
D_{16i} &= (w_i^{-r_2/t_i})^{s_{2i}} = w_i^{-r_2 s_{2i}/t_i} \\
&= w_i^{-r_2(-a_i t_i \cdot r_2^{-1})/t_i} \\
&= w_i^{a_i} \\
&= w_i^{-r_1(-a_i t_i \cdot r_1^{-1})/t_i} \\
&= w_i^{-r_1 s_{1i}/t_i} \\
&= (w_i^{-r_1/t_i})^{s_{1i}} = D_{26i}.
\end{aligned}$$

Lastly, the result follows by

$$D_{15} \cdot D_{161} \cdots D_{16n} \cdot \mu = g^\gamma \cdot w_1^{a_1} \cdots w_n^{a_n} \cdot g^\beta$$

$$= g^{-\alpha \cdot (a_1 + \cdots + a_n) - \beta} \cdot u_1^{a_1} \cdots u_n^{a_n} \cdot v^{\sum_{i=1}^n a_i} \cdot g^\beta$$

$$= u_1^{a_1} \cdots u_n^{a_n} \cdot g^{-\alpha \cdot (\sum_{i=1}^n a_i)} \cdot g^{-\beta} \cdot g^{\alpha(\sum_{i=1}^n a_i)} \cdot g^\beta$$

$$= u_1^{a_1} \cdots u_n^{a_n}.$$

Full Verifiability. Assume without loss of generality that $\mathcal{U}_1$ is a malicious server, i.e. it deviates from its functionality to cheat $\mathcal{C}$ with a non-negligible probability, that is InvDel is not fully verifiable. Since $\mathcal{U}_1$ is honest, any manipulation of D_{1j} can be fully detected by $\mathcal{C}$ using the values D_{2j}, $j = 2, 3, 4$ in the first verification step. This implies that $\mathcal{U}_2$ is required to manipulate at least one of the results D_{11i}, $1 \le i \le n$, to pass the second verification step. The reason is that after a correct execution of the first step, any manipulation of D_{15} or D_{16i}, $1 \le i \le n$, can be fully detected by $\mathcal{C}$ since $\mathcal{U}_2$ is honest; hence $\mathcal{U}_1$ cannot pass the verification with a maliciously generated output by Congruence (6). Therefore, there exists *at least one* k with $1 \le k \le n$ for which $\mathcal{U}_1$ manipulates D_{11k} with an element $X \ne D_{11k}$. Note that X is maliciously chosen by $\mathcal{U}_1$, which can also be chosen by inspecting the single or multiple executions of InvDel and using any maliciously chosen inputs/outputs. Then, $\mathcal{C}$ computes

$$Y = X \cdot R_1 = X \cdot g^{r_1}$$

instead of $w_1^{-r_1/t_k} = D_{11k} \cdot R_1$ by following the description of InvDel. Note however that $\mathcal{U}_1$ cannot compute r_1 even if it has an unrestricted computational power since the value Y is not given to $\mathcal{U}_1$, and r_1 is chosen arbitrarily random from $\mathbb{Z}_q^*$ in the precomputation step Rand. Then, $\mathcal{C}$ delegates the computation of

$$Z_1 = Y^{s_{1k}} = X^{s_{1k}} g^{s_{1k} r_1}$$

instead of the correct value $D_{26k} = (D_{11k} \cdot R_1)^{s_{1k}}$ to $\mathcal{U}_2$. Note that Z_1 is computed correctly as $\mathcal{U}_2$ is honest. On the other side, $\mathcal{U}_1$ can also compute Z_1 since it can pass the verification step with its inputs and X with a non-negligible probability due to the above discussion. In other words, $\mathcal{U}_1$ can compute

$$X^{a_k t_k r_1^{-1}} g^{-a_k t_k}.$$

This means in particular that $\mathcal{U}_1$ must *necessarily*[2] know the value of $a_k t_k$, which is however randomly chosen by $\mathcal{C}$ from $\mathbb{Z}_q^*$ in the precomputation step Rand, and protected from $\mathcal{U}_1$. This is because of the fact that s_{1k} is only known by the honest server $\mathcal{U}_2$; hence t_1 is protected from $\mathcal{U}_1$. This gives us a contradiction of the claim that $\mathcal{U}_1$ can deviate from its functionality with a non-negligible probability. Analogously, any attempt to manipulate D_{26i}, $1 \leq i \leq n$ with $k \neq i$, leads also to a contradiction to the claim that $\mathcal{U}_1$ can deviate from its functionality with a non-negligible probability by the same reasoning. Therefore, InvDel is fully verifiable.

Security. We assume now that $\mathcal{A} = (\mathcal{E}, \mathcal{U}_1', \mathcal{U}_2')$ is a PPT adversary interacting with a PPT-based algorithm $\mathcal{C}$ in the delegated-security definitions of Sect. 2 under the OMTUP-model. Our first claim is

$$EVIEW_{real} \sim EVIEW_{ideal},$$

in particular, Pair One holds in the security model of Sect. 2. i.e. the *external* adversary environment $\mathcal{E}$ cannot learn anything useful.

If the inputs $((a_1, a_2, \cdots, a_n), (u_1, u_2, \cdots, u_n))$ are either honest, protected or adversarial, protected, then a simulator $\mathcal{S}_1$ behaves exactly as in the real execution, i.e. it never requires to access the input elements, and there is nothing to prove as the inputs

$$((a_1, a_2, \cdots, a_n), (u_1, u_2, \cdots, u_n)) \in (\mathbb{Z}_q^*)^n \times \mathbb{G}^n$$

are not secret to the adversary $\mathcal{E}$. We assume now that the inputs are honest, secret inputs. Then, ignoring the ith round, the simulator $\mathcal{S}_1$ first chooses elements $\ell_i, \eta_i \in \mathbb{Z}_q^*$, $h_i, k_i \in \mathbb{G}$, $1 \leq i \leq n$, and $\tau_j, \varphi_j \in \mathbb{Z}_q^*$, $1 \leq j \leq 3$, randomly, and makes $n + 3$ random queries to $\mathcal{U}_1'$

---

[2] Even though it is not sufficient to cheat $\mathcal{C}$ with a non-negligible probability.

- $\mathcal{U}_1(\ell_i, h_i) \longleftarrow D_{11i} = h_i^{\ell_i}$ for $1 \leq i \leq n$,
- $\mathcal{U}_1(\cdot^{-1}, \tau_j) \longleftarrow D_{12} = \tau_j^{-1}$ for $1 \leq j \leq 3$

and $n + 3$ random queries to $\mathcal{U}_2'$

- $\mathcal{U}_2(\eta_i, k_i) \longleftarrow D_{21i} = k_i^{\eta_i}$ for $1 \leq i \leq n$,
- $\mathcal{U}_2(\cdot^{-1}, \varphi_j) \longleftarrow D_{22} = \varphi_j^{-1}$ for $1 \leq j \leq 3$.

After receiving the outputs of $\mathcal{U}_1'$ and $\mathcal{U}_2'$, $\mathcal{S}_1$ chooses randomly $m_i, n_i \in \mathbb{G}$, $\omega_i, \zeta_i \in \mathbb{Z}_q^*$, $1 \leq i \leq 4$, $g_1, g_2 \in \mathbb{G}$, and $\tau_4, \varphi_4 \in \mathbb{Z}_q^*$, and queries randomly to $\mathcal{U}_1'$

- $\mathcal{U}_1(\tau_4, g_1) \longleftarrow D_{15} = g_1^{\tau_4}$,
- $\mathcal{U}_1(\omega_i, m_i) \longleftarrow D_{16i} = m_i^{\omega_i}$ for $1 \leq i \leq n$,

similarly, $\mathcal{S}_1$ queries randomly to $\mathcal{U}_2'$

- $\mathcal{U}_2(\varphi_4, g_2) \longleftarrow D_{25} = g_2^{\varphi_4}$,
- $\mathcal{U}_2(\zeta_i, n_i) \longleftarrow D_{26i} = n_i^{\zeta_i}$ for $1 \leq i \leq n$.

Then, $\mathcal{S}_1$ behaves as follows:

- If the outputs D_{1j} of $\mathcal{U}_1'$ and D_{2j} of $\mathcal{U}_1'$ are not equal for a randomly selected j, $2 \leq j \leq 5$; or if D_{16i} of $\mathcal{U}_1'$ and D_{26i} of $\mathcal{U}_2'$ are not equal for a randomly selected i, $1 \leq i \leq n$, then the values $Y_p^i = $ "error", $Y_u^i = \emptyset$, and $replace^i = 1$ (corresponding to the output $(estate^i, \text{"error"}, \emptyset)$ in the ideal process) are produced by $\mathcal{S}_1$,
- if no "error" is detected , then the values $Y_p^i = \emptyset$, $Y_u^i = \emptyset$, and $replace^i = 0$ (corresponding to the output $(estate^i, Y_p^i, Y_u^i)$ in the ideal process) are produced by $\mathcal{S}_1$,
- otherwise, $\mathcal{S}_1$ selects a random element r and outputs $Y_p^i = r$, $Y_u^i = \emptyset$, and $replace^i = 1$ (corresponding to the output $(estate^i, r, Y_u^i)$ in the ideal process).

In either cases, $\mathcal{S}_1$ saves the appropriate states.

The distributions of inputs in the real and ideal experiments are computationally indistinguishable. In the ideal experiment, the inputs are chosen uniformly at random. In the real experiment, all inputs of InvDel are independently randomized by the choice of uniformly distributed random elements (in practice via the precomputation step Rand). Note that, by each invocation of InvDel, new random values are generated by Rand which are different from other invocations, and computationally indistinguishable from random elements. Now, since InvDel is fully verifiable, we have only two cases:

- If $\mathcal{U}_1'$ and $\mathcal{U}_2'$ behave honestly both in the real and the ideal experiments in the round i, then we have $EVIEW_{real}^i \sim EVIEW_{ideal}^i$ since in the real execution $\mathcal{C}^{\mathcal{U}_1', \mathcal{U}_2'}$ runs InvDel perfectly, and in the ideal execution $\mathcal{S}_1$ does not change the output,
- If one of $\mathcal{U}_1'$ or $\mathcal{U}_2'$ behaves dishonestly in the round i, than this can be fully detected by both $\mathcal{C}$ and $\mathcal{S}_1$ because of the full verifiability of InvDel.

In particular, it is impossible that InvDel could be corrupted which implies that $\mathcal{S}_1$ never executes the third case above, i.e. it does not select a random element r and return consequently $Y_p^i = r$, $Y_u^i = \emptyset$, and $replace^i = 1$ in the ideal experiment. More precisely, this observation implies that it is impossible that both $\mathcal{U}_1'$ and $\mathcal{U}_2'$ deviate from their functionalities at the same time. Thus, we have

$$EVIEW_{real}^i \sim EVIEW_{ideal}^i$$

even in the case that one of $\mathcal{U}_i'$, $i = 1, 2$, misbehaves. By the hybrid argument, we conclude the first result

$$EVIEW_{real} \sim EVIEW_{ideal}.$$

It is clear that this argument only works if *only* one server misbehaves (under the OMTUP-model), i.e. if both $\mathcal{U}_1$ and $\mathcal{U}_2$ are malicious at the same time, then the misbehavior in this case is *not* independent of the inputs whereas the misbehavior of only one of $\mathcal{U}_i$, i=1,2, is independent of the inputs.

Secondly, we show that

$$UVIEW_{real} \sim UVIEW_{ideal}.$$

In particular, Pair Two holds in the security model of Sect. 2, i.e. the malicious server $\mathcal{U}_i$, $i = 1$ or $i = 2$, learns nothing useful under the OMTUP-model. For a round i, a simulator $\mathcal{S}_2$ behaves exactly like $\mathcal{S}_1$ to produce random queries by ignoring the ith round for both $\mathcal{U}_1'$ and $\mathcal{U}_2'$, and saves its states. Furthermore, it saves the states of $(\mathcal{U}_1', \mathcal{U}_2')$. An external environment adversary can tell neither to $\mathcal{U}_1'$ nor to $\mathcal{U}_2'$ that $\mathcal{S}_2$ produces corrupted outputs since the output in the real experiment is not corrupted, and neither $\mathcal{E}$ and $\mathcal{U}_1'$ nor $\mathcal{E}$ and $\mathcal{U}_2'$ are capable of communicating with each other directly to be able to develop a joint strategy after interacting with $\mathcal{C}$ once (by the fundamental assumption of Sect. 2). Hence, honest, secret; honest, protected; or adversarial, protected inputs are all private for both $\mathcal{U}_1'$ and $\mathcal{U}_2'$, although $\mathcal{E}$ is capable of easily distinguishing between these real and ideal experiments. The reason is that in the ith round of the real experiment, the values given to either $\mathcal{U}_1'$ or $\mathcal{U}_2'$ are randomized by Rand, whereas $\mathcal{S}_2$ generates random, independent queries for both $\mathcal{U}_1'$ and $\mathcal{U}_2'$ in the ideal experiment exactly as in the case of interacting with $\mathcal{S}_1$. Hence,

$$UVIEW_{real}^i \sim UVIEW_{ideal}^i$$

holds for each round i. It follows then (analogous to Pair One) by a hybrid argument that

$$UVIEW_{real} \sim UVIEW_{ideal}.$$

Efficiency. InvDel requires

- $n + 1$ **MMs** to compute w_i and γ, $1 \le i \le n$,
- n **MIs** to compute t_i^{-1}, $1 \le i \le n$,
- $3 \cdot n + 3$ **MMs** to finish the first queries,

Table 1. Comparison of the delegator's computational costs and communication complexities.

	# Servers	$\approx$ # MMs Org. Sch.	$\approx$ # MMs Ver. ≥ 0.9 Del. Inv.	# Rounds Del. Inv.	Verf.
[10] TC'05	2	509	$\log_2 10 \cdot 19 \approx$ 63	$1 + 1 = 2$	1/2
[6] ESORICS'12	2	307	$\log_3 10 \cdot 13 \approx$ 27	$1 + 1 = 2$	2/3
[19] ESORICS'14 ($\chi = 2^{64}$)	1	508	$\log_2 10 \cdot 116 \approx$ 385	$1 + 1 = 2$	1/2
[11] IJIS'16 (with $c = 4$)	1	200	102	$2 + 1 = 3$	9/10
[15] AsiaCCS'16	2	513	23	$2 + 1 = 3$	1
InvDel (with $n = 1$)	2	21	21	2	1

- $2 \cdot n + 6$ **MMs** to prepare the second round of queries,
- one **MM** to compute $\gamma \cdot \ell^{-1}$,
- $n + 1$ **MMs** to recover $u_1^{a_1} \cdots u_n^{a_n}$.

Furthermore, computation of modular exponentiations takes $\mathcal{O}(\log q)$ steps (e.g. by the square-and-multiply method). Hence, $(\mathcal{C}, \mathcal{U}_1, \mathcal{U}_2)$ is an $\mathcal{O}(1/\log q)$-efficient implementation of InvDel. This completes the proof. $\square$

Remark 2 The discussion in Sect. 3.2 implies that computations of n different **MI**s can be replaced by $2n$ **MMs** by delegating the computation of t_i^{-1}, $1 \leq i \leq n$, in a previous call of InvDel. Hence, the overall computational cost of InvDel corresponds to $9n + 12$ **MMs**, and does not require any computation of **MI**s. Since we only have 21 **MMs** for $n = 1$, we perform $(21n - (9n + 12)) + (n - 1) = 13n - 14$ less **MMs** by means of n-simultaneous delegation via InvDel than individual delegations of **GE**s n different times (i.e. delegating the computation of each $u_1^{a_1}, \cdots, u_n^{a_n}$ separately, and combining them with $n - 1$ **MMs** in order to recover the simultaneous group exponentiation $u_1^{a_1} \cdots u_n^{a_n}$).

4   Comparison and Implementation Results

In this section, we give a comparative efficiency analysis of InvDel with the previous schemes [6, 10, 11, 15] together with its implementation results.

First column of Table 1 gives whether the schemes are introduced using a single untrusted server or under the OMTUP assumption. We assume that a single modular inversion approximately requires 100 **MMs** [11], and give the approximate number of required **MMs** accordingly in the second column of Table 1 to compare the total computational cost of $\mathcal{C}$ in different schemes with InvDel. Third column of Table 1 gives the approximate number of required **MMs** of different schemes if the computation of **MI**s are also delegated like in InvDel. This means that each **MI** corresponds to two **MMs** via delegating its computation as in InvDel. To give a fair comparison, we count the approximate number of required **MMs** by the verification probability of at least 9/10. For example, [10] requires 5 **MIs** and 9 **MMs** corresponding to $5 \cdot 2 + 9 = 19$ **MMs** with a verifiability probability 1/2 if **MIs** are delegated[3]. Therefore, [10] requires $\log_2 10 \cdot 19 \approx 63$ **MMs** if the verifiability probability is 9/10 and **MIs** are delegated like in InvDel. Similarly, other results [6,15,19] are compared with InvDel in the third column with increasing the verification probability to at least 9/10 if necessary. Fourth column of Table 1 gives the number of rounds if **MIs** are also delegated. Note that all the schemes except InvDel require an *additional round* of communication since **MIs** are required in their first rounds in contrast to InvDel; InvDel requires **MIs** first in the second round and the computation can be delegated in the first round without increasing the total number of rounds. The last column of Table 1 gives the comparison of verifiability probabilities of a single delegation. In summary, Table 1 shows that InvDel (already with $n = 1$) is by far the most computationally efficient delegation scheme requiring only 21 **MMs** and no **MIs** computations by $\mathcal{C}$ while providing full verifiability.

Table 2. CPU cost: InvDel vs. local computation

Moduli size	InvDel cost (ms)	Local computation cost (ms)	Gain factor
2048-bit	1	174	≈ 174
3072-bit	3	567	≈ 189
4092-bit	6	1322	≈ 220.33
7680-bit	18	8548	≈ 474.88
15360-bit	67	107419	≈ 1603.26

In order to confirm the theoretical efficiency analysis of InvDel in practice in a mobile setting, we developed an application for Android devices. In this application, various delegation schemes are implemented simultaneously. The application requires at least an android version 6.0 to carry out the implementation of different schemes and document the required time at each execution. In order to efficiently perform the underlying cryptographic operations, we have implemented the application by using the MIRACL library [13] for fast arithmetic. The results regarding the time cost are carried out by utilizing a Samsung Galaxy J3 (2017) smartphone with an 1.4 GHz quad core processor and 2 GB RAM, where the android operating system version 7.0 is run. We create the implementation results with various security levels corresponding to different bit lengths for the prime modulus varying from 2048 bits to 15360 bits corresponding to the security levels varying from 112 bits to 256 bits.

---

[3] [15] requires 3 **MIs** and 13 **MMs**, whereas the preprocessing step requires for each delegation 2 more **MIs** which was not counted in [15], however it required to be added to the total cost in Table 1 to give a fair comparison.

Table 2 compares the computational CPU costs of InvDel (for $n = 1$) with the corresponding local computation of a **GE** at various security levels. It also gives the gain factor if C uses InvDel instead of computing a single **GE** locally.

Figure 1 gives a comparative analysis of the implementation results of various schemes proposed under the OMTUP assumption using our Android application. More precisely, we compare InvDel with $n = 1$ with the scheme of Hohenberger and Lysyanskaya [10] with a verification probability $1/2$ (**TC'05**), the scheme of Chen et al. [6] with a verification probability $2/3$ (**ESORICS'12**), and the fully verifiable scheme of Ren et al. [15] (**AsiaCCS'16**). These implementation results at different security levels also validate our theoretical analysis in the practice that InvDel outperforms even the schemes which do not satisfy full verifiability when used in a resource-constrained device like a smart phone.

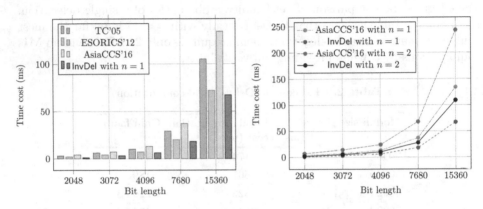

Fig. 1. Comparison of implementation results

Fig. 2. Comparison of fully verif. schemes

Figure 2 compares the computational efficiency of the fully verifiable scheme of Ren et al. [15] for $n = 1$, and 2-simultaneous scheme in [15] with a *corrected* verifiability probability $5/6$ for $n = 2$ (see the attack in [18, Sect. 3.2]) with InvDel (for $n = 1, 2$). It shows that InvDel has much better performance than the schemes in [15]. Furthermore, it can be seen in Fig. 2 that the higher the security level will be, the better the advantage of InvDel becomes.

5   Delegated Schnorr's Signature Scheme

In this section we utilize InvDel to propose a delegation-secure verification for Schnorr's signatures following [6,10]. Our delegation-secure variant of the verification step for Schnorr's signatures consists of the following steps:

– **System Parameters Generation:** Let p and q be two large primes satisfying $q|p - 1$. Let g be a fixed element in $\mathbb{Z}_p^*$ of order q. Let further a cryptographic secure hash function $H : \{0,1\}^* \to \mathbb{Z}_p$ be given. The system parameters are given as $SP = \{p, q, g, H\}$.

- **Key Generation:** On the input σ (as is Sect. 2), run an key generation algorithm KeyGen to obtain the pair of signing and verification keys (x, y) with $y = g^{-x} \mod p$.
- **Signature Generation:** On the input x and a message m, the signer $\mathcal{S}$ computes a pair $(k, r = g^k \mod p)$ and $e = H(m \| r)$, $s = k + xe \mod q$, and outputs the signature $\sigma = (e, s)$.
- **Signature Verification:** On the input y, the message m, and the signature $\sigma = (e, s)$, the delegator $\mathcal{C}$ runs subroutine InvDel (with $n = 2$), and verifies the signature σ as follows:
    1. $\mathcal{C}$ runs $\mathsf{InvDel}((s, e), (g, y))$
       $\leftarrow (\psi_1 = g^s, \psi_2 = y^e)^4$.
    2. $\mathcal{C}$ computes $r' = \psi_1 \psi_2 \mod p$ and
       $e' = H(m \| r')$.
    3. $\mathcal{C}$ outputs 1 if $e' = e$. Otherwise, $\mathcal{C}_2$ outputs $\perp$.

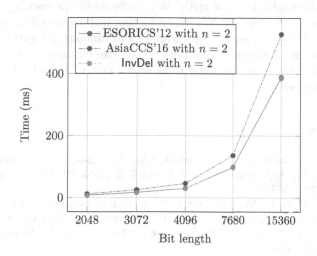

Fig. 3. Delegation-secure Schnorr's signatures

Figure 3 compares the implementation results of the delegated Schnorr's signatures using InvDel ($n = 2$) with the delegated Schnorr's signatures using the schemes in [6,15] showing that InvDel (with $n = 2$) outperforms even the most efficient schemes [6,15] with low verifiability probabilities $1/2$ and $5/6$ with $n = 2$, respectively, while providing full verifiability.

---

[4] Since the values g and y are public, one can use a simpler variant of InvDel in which these bases are not required to be blinded before the delegation in order to further improve the efficiency of the verification step. However, we randomize both the exponents and the bases following the previous works [6,10] since it is usually a privacy requirement that the external servers obtain no useful information about the inputs, even the public ones.

6   Conclusion

Main goal of this study is to address the problem of fully verifiable secure delegation of simultaneous **GE**s. We propose an efficient, fully verifiable and secure delegation scheme InvDel for simultaneous **GE**s. We then implement InvDel on various security levels in a mobile application environment. Both our theoretical efficiency analysis and the implementation results show that InvDel is the most efficient secure delegation scheme providing full verifiability when compared with the previous ones. For instance, our implementation results show that increasing 5-times the bit size of the modulus from 3072-bits to 15360-bits yields to the increasing the gain factor of delegation from 189-times to more than 1603-times (e.g. the relative factor will be 8.49, much better than only 5-times). In particular, the more the security level is, the better the advantage of InvDel becomes if carefully compared with the previous delegation schemes or the local computation. Furthermore, we gain a linear factor in n (e.g. $8n - 8$ less modular multiplications) if n-simultaneous **GE**s are delegated with InvDel improving the efficiency of the applications of InvDel in cryptographic protocols which require multiple **GE**s simultaneously. We illustrate this fact by speeding-up the verification step of Schnorr's signatures using 2-simultaneous delegation via InvDel. As possible future works, it is desirable to propose efficient fully verifiable delegation schemes for (simultaneous) **GE**s under the TUP and OUP-models, or prove their impossibilities.

References

1. Agnew, G.B., Mullin, R.C., Onyszchuk, I.M., Vanstone, S.A.: An implementation for a fast public-key cryptosystem. J. Cryptol. **3**(2), 63–79 (1991). https://doi.org/10.1007/BF00196789
2. Boyko, V., Peinado, M., Venkatesan, R.: Speeding up discrete log and factoring based schemes via precomputations. In: Nyberg, K. (ed.) EUROCRYPT 1998. LNCS, vol. 1403, pp. 221–235. Springer, Heidelberg (1998). https://doi.org/10.1007/BFb0054129
3. Brickell, E.F., Gordon, D.M., McCurley, K.S., Wilson, D.B.: Fast exponentiation with precomputation. In: Rueppel, R.A. (ed.) EUROCRYPT 1992. LNCS, vol. 658, pp. 200–207. Springer, Heidelberg (1993). https://doi.org/10.1007/3-540-47555-9_18
4. Cavallo, B., Di Crescenzo, G., Kahrobaei, D., Shpilrain, V.: Efficient and secure delegation of group exponentiation to a single server. In: Mangard, S., Schaumont, P. (eds.) RFIDSec 2015. LNCS, vol. 9440, pp. 156–173. Springer, Cham (2015). https://doi.org/10.1007/978-3-319-24837-0_10
5. Chaum, D., Pedersen, T.P.: Wallet databases with observers. In: Brickell, E.F. (ed.) CRYPTO 1992. LNCS, vol. 740, pp. 89–105. Springer, Heidelberg (1993). https://doi.org/10.1007/3-540-48071-4_7
6. Chen, X., Li, J., Ma, J., Tang, Q., Lou, W.: New algorithms for secure outsourcing of modular exponentiations. In: Foresti, S., Yung, M., Martinelli, F. (eds.) ESORICS 2012. LNCS, vol. 7459, pp. 541–556. Springer, Heidelberg (2012). https://doi.org/10.1007/978-3-642-33167-1_31

7. Chevalier, C., Laguillaumie, F., Vergnaud, D.: Privately outsourcing exponentiation to a single server: cryptanalysis and optimal constructions. In: Askoxylakis, I., Ioannidis, S., Katsikas, S., Meadows, C. (eds.) ESORICS 2016. LNCS, vol. 9878, pp. 261–278. Springer, Cham (2016). https://doi.org/10.1007/978-3-319-45744-4_13

8. Galbraith, S.D.: Mathematics of Public Key Cryptography, 1st edn. Cambridge University Press, New York (2012). https://doi.org/10.1017/CBO9781139012843

9. Gentry, C.: Fully homomorphic encryption using ideal lattices. In: Proceedings of the Forty-first Annual ACM Symposium on Theory of Computing, STOC 2009, pp. 169–178. ACM, New York (2009). https://doi.org/10.1145/1536414.1536440

10. Hohenberger, S., Lysyanskaya, A.: How to securely outsource cryptographic computations. In: Kilian, J. (ed.) TCC 2005. LNCS, vol. 3378, pp. 264–282. Springer, Heidelberg (2005). https://doi.org/10.1007/978-3-540-30576-7_15

11. Kiraz, M.S., Uzunkol, O.: Efficient and verifiable algorithms for secure outsourcing of cryptographic computations. Int. J. Inf. Secur. **15**(5), 519–537 (2016). https://doi.org/10.1007/s10207-015-0308-7

12. Kuppusamy, L., Rangasamy, J.: CRT-based outsourcing algorithms for modular exponentiations. In: Dunkelman, O., Sanadhya, S.K. (eds.) INDOCRYPT 2016. LNCS, vol. 10095, pp. 81–98. Springer, Cham (2016). https://doi.org/10.1007/978-3-319-49890-4_5

13. Ltd., S.S.: MIRACL Users Manual (2006). https://github.com/miracl/MIRACL

14. M'Raïhi, D., Naccache, D.: Batch exponentiation: a fast DLP-based signature generation strategy. In: Proceedings of the 3rd ACM Conference on Computer and Communications Security, CCS 1996, pp. 58–61. ACM, New York (1996). https://doi.org/10.1145/238168.238187

15. Ren, Y., Ding, N., Zhang, X., Lu, H., Gu, D.: Verifiable outsourcing algorithms for modular exponentiations with improved checkability. In: Proceedings of the 11th ACM on Asia Conference on Computer and Communications Security, AsiaCCS 2016, pp. 293–303. ACM, New York (2016). https://doi.org/10.1145/2897845.2897881

16. Schroeppel, R., Orman, H., O'Malley, S., Spatscheck, O.: Fast key exchange with elliptic curve systems. In: Coppersmith, D. (ed.) CRYPTO 1995. LNCS, vol. 963, pp. 43–56. Springer, Heidelberg (1995). https://doi.org/10.1007/3-540-44750-4_4

17. Uzunkol, O., Kalkar, O., Sertkaya, I.: Fully verifiable secure delegation of pairing computation: cryptanalysis and an efficient construction. Cryptology ePrint Archive, Report 2017/1173 (2017). https://eprint.iacr.org/2017/1173

18. Uzunkol, O., Rangasamy, J., Kuppusamy, L.: Hide the Modulus: a secure non-interactive fully verifiable delegation scheme for modular exponentiations via CRT. In: Chen, L., Manulis, M., Schneider, S. (eds.) ISC 2018. LNCS, vol. 11060, pp. 250–267. Springer, Cham (2018). https://doi.org/10.1007/978-3-319-99136-8_14

19. Wang, Y., et al.: Securely outsourcing exponentiations with single untrusted program for cloud storage. In: Kutyłowski, M., Vaidya, J. (eds.) ESORICS 2014. LNCS, vol. 8712, pp. 326–343. Springer, Cham (2014). https://doi.org/10.1007/978-3-319-11203-9_19

20. Yao, A.C.: Protocols for secure computations. In: 23rd Annual Symposium on Foundations of Computer Science (sfcs 1982) (FOCS), pp. 160–164 (1982). https://doi.org/10.1109/SFCS.1982.88

21. Zhou, K., Afifi, M.H., Ren, J.: ExpSOS: secure and verifiable outsourcing of exponentiation operations for mobile cloud computing. IEEE Trans. Inf. Forensics Secur. **12**(11), 2518–2531 (2017). https://doi.org/10.1109/TIFS.2017.2710941

An Efficient Framework for Improved Task Offloading in Edge Computing

Amanjot Kaur[1](✉) and Ramandeep Kaur[2](✉)

[1] Department of Computer Science and Engineering,
Chandigarh University, Mohali, India
amantung521@gmail.com
[2] Department of Computer Science, Shahzadanand College,
Maqbool road, Amritsar 143001, India
rdhillon1223@gmail.com

Abstract. In cloud environment the efficient techniques to balance the load are needed to equally distribute the load between available data centers to save some of the nodes from getting over loaded while others getting lightly loaded or free. The loads in cloud data centers should be mapped on to available resources in such a way that energy utilization in edge computing should be optimized. With the use of load balancing, utilization of resources can be optimized which can significantly decrease energy consumption and can even reduce carbon release along with cooling necessities in cloud data centers. In this paper, a novel game theoretic approach has been proposed to improve the throughput of the edge computing. Also, an effort is made to reduce the energy consumed during the offloading in the edge computing. Extensive analysis shows that the performance of proposed technique consumes lesser energy and provide faster response to edge users.

Keywords: Edge computing · Energy consumption · Offloading
Delay

1 Introduction

From the perspective of mobile devices, the demands of latency critical and computing intensive applications are increased i.e., AR/VR, multimedia IoT based cooperative video processing. These applications are hoped to be executed with both lower latency and less energy consumption over the mobile devices, to win better user experience. However, due to the constraints of cost, size and weight at the mobile device, its computing capability and energy supply are restricted [1], and the technique breakthrough seems unpredictable in the near future [2]. From the perspective of IoTs, the development of Internet-of-Everything (IoE) brings massive IoT based cloud connection requests. Though the remote cloud has abundant computing and storage resources, its access capability is poor. It is predicted by Cisco that at the end of 2020, about 50 billion IoT devices (sensors, or wearable devices) need to interact with the cloud [3]. On the one hand,

© Springer Nature Switzerland AG 2018
I. Traore et al. (Eds.): ISDDC 2018, LNCS 11317, pp. 94–101, 2018.
https://doi.org/10.1007/978-3-030-03712-3_8

the large number of cloud connections will cause the congestion of backhaul, on the other hand, the remote cloud service requests from these devices have to cross the wide area network (WAN), thus it is difficult to promise the delay and jitter based quality-of-service (QoS). From the perspective of operators, though their investments and the amount of network traffic are increasing, their developed networks are gradually channelized and the average revenue per user (ARPU) is constantly decrease [4].

In order to overcome above contradictions, a new technology named mobile edge computing (MEC) is proposed [5,6] and it is known to be one of the key tools for the coming 5G. In essence, MEC is a novel paradigm who extends the centralized cloud computing capabilities to the edge of cloud. OpenFog Consortium and standard development organizations like ETSI have also recognized the benefits that the MEC can bring to consumers [7]. In particular, it is noted that MEC is becoming an important enabler of consumer-centric applications and services that demand real-time operations, e.g., smart mobility, connected vehicles, smart cities, and location based services.

In this paper, the delay-energy-cost tradeoff based offloading cost is proposed to quantify the user-perceived performance of the task offloading, and then it is used to conduct the jointly task offloading decision and resource allocation. Moreover, the edge server access-cost depends on both the associated access point and accessed edge server, and which reflects the different edge server access delay and service (or resource using) cost negotiated by access points and edge servers. At last, both problems of minimizing the sum of offloading cost for all edge users (efficiency-based) and minimizing the maximal offloading cost per edge user (fairness-based) are formulated.

In the rest of the paper, we first present the architecture of an Edge system and give an overview of our game-theoretic framework in Sect. 2. Then in Sects. 3, we describe task distribution mechanisms and revenue sharing mechanisms. Section 4 presents our findings via experiments and simulations, and we conclude the paper in Sect. 5.

2 Edge System

In this section, we first discuss background and related work, and then we give an overview of an Edge system.

2.1 Architecture

There are three types of entities in an edge computing as: (1) Clients, including applications and end users, that are at the edge of the Internet and submit computing tasks to the system. (2) Edge providers (computing service providers at the edge of the Internet and close to clients, and hence have high communication bandwidth and low propagation delay to clients), and cloud providers (providers in the cloud that offer servers to edge clients by joining an Edge system). (3) A system manager, which is a software component that implements mechanisms/algorithms for various management issues such as facilitating task submissions, revenue collection from clients, revenue split among servers, accounting/auditing, etc. The main part of the manager resides on the edge and some of its components are distributed among providers throughout the Internet. In the system, clients communicate with and submit their tasks to the system manager through apps on their devices.

2.2 Proposed Framework

We assume that the two types of mechanisms (i.e., task distribution and revenue sharing) work on individual servers, without any consideration of the identities of the owners (i.e., providers) of those servers, as the objectives of those system-level mechanisms are to optimally utilize available *servers* to maximize total received revenue and fairly distribute the revenue[1] among participating *servers*. Those mechanisms are publicly known to all clients and service providers. Under those mechanisms, a service provider attempts to maximize its received benefit or utility (defined below) by strategically adjusting the computing resources it provides to the system.

A utility function captures the tradeoff between the revenue and the cost of a provider. Providing more servers will incur more cost to a provider, even though more servers imply more revenue that the provider can potentially receive. Then the utility function of a provider p can be described as

$$U_p(n_p) = v_p(n_p) - f_{cost}(n_p) \tag{1}$$

where $v_p(n_p)$ is the revenue received by provider p when placing n_p servers in the system, and the cost f_{cost} is an increasing function of the number of servers. We focus on a linear cost function $f_{cost}(n_p) = \alpha_p n_p$ with $\alpha_p > 0$.

The edge player and the cloud player attempt to solve the following optimization problems respectively

$$\max_{n_E} U_E(n_E, n_C) = v_E(M_{share}(M_{opt}(n_E, n_C))) - \alpha_E n_E$$

$$\max_{n_C} U_C(n_C, n_E) = v_C(M_{share}(M_{opt}(n_E, n_C))) - \alpha_C n_C$$

The Nash equilibrium is denoted by

$$\{n_E^*, n_C^*\} \tag{2}$$

where $n_E^* = \text{argmax}_{n_E} U_E(n_E, n_C^*)$ and $n_C^* = \text{argmax}_{n_C} U_C(n_C, n_E^*)$. Note that the definition (2) can be easily generalized to the definition of a Nash equilibrium of a m-player game: $\{n_i^*\}, \forall i \in \{1, 2, \ldots, m\}$ with $n_i^* = \text{argmax}_{n_i} U_i(n_i, n_{-i}^*)$ (where $-i$ denotes the set of all players except i).

---

[1] A system manager may keep a share of the total received revenue and split the rest among servers. We assume that a system manager's own revenue share is negligible compared with the rest of the revenue given to servers.

3   Mechanism for Distributing Computing Tasks

In this section, we discuss mechanisms that distribute tasks of edge clients to the servers in an Edge system.

3.1   Objective of Task Distribution

Since an important application of edge computing is to serve tasks with low latency requirement, we focus on tasks with completion deadlines. Recall that a task has a value, which can be regarded as the payment that the task's owner (i.e., a client) is willing to pay for completing the task [8]. *The objective of a task distribution mechanism is to maximize the total received value (as a revenue) for the tasks that are completed before their deadlines.* In this section, we present an optimization formulation for the case where tasks arrive in a batch (i.e., at the same time) to illustrate the characteristic of task distribution, and then we will present a greedy algorithm to address a practical dynamic task arrival setting [9].

3.2   Optimal Task Offloading

Let $\mathbb{N}_J$ denote the set of tasks with $N_J = |\mathbb{N}_J|$, and let $\mathbb{N}_S$ denote the set of servers with $N_S = |\mathbb{N}_S|$ [10]. Tasks are ordered increasingly according to their arrival times and indexed by $i = 1, \ldots, N_J$, and servers are indexed by $j = 1, \ldots, N_S$ [11]. Let x_{ij} denote the assignment of task i to server j. Then $x_{ij} = 1$ represents that task i is assigned to server j; otherwise $x_{ij} = 0$. Let d_{ij} denote the completion time of task i when it is assigned to server j. Note that d_{ij} includes the computation time of task i on server j and the time to transfer task i to server j. In addition, a task i might experience a queuing delay if some other tasks are scheduled on the same sever (as task i) but should be executed before task i as they arrive earlier than task i. Queuing delay is discussed next [12].

Let v_i denote the value of task i or the payment that the owner (i.e., client) of task i will pay for completing task i. If task i is completed before its deadline, the system manager will receive v_i; otherwise, the manager receives nothing. The objective of the manager is to maximize its total received payment or value (as a revenue) by solving the following optimization problem [13].

$$\max_{x_{ij}} \quad \sum_{j=1}^{N_S} \sum_{i=1}^{N_J} v_i x_{ij} \tag{3}$$

$$s.t. \qquad 0 \leqslant \sum_{j=1}^{N_S} x_{ij} \leqslant 1, \quad \forall i \tag{4}$$

$$x_{ij} \in \{0,1\}, \forall i; \forall j \tag{5}$$

$$x_{ij} d_{ij} + \sum_{k=1}^{i-1} q_{ijk} d_{kj} \leqslant L_i, \quad \forall i, \forall j \tag{6}$$

$$x_{ij} = 0 \rightarrow q_{ijk} = 0, \forall i, \forall k \in \{1, \ldots, i-1\}; \forall j \tag{7}$$

$$x_{ij} = 1 \rightarrow q_{ijk} = x_{kj}, \forall i, \forall k \in \{1, \ldots, i-1\}; \forall j \tag{8}$$

$$q_{ijk} \in \{0,1\}, \forall i, \forall k \in \{1, \ldots, i-1\}; \forall j \tag{9}$$

where (4) and (5) say that a task can be assigned to at most one server. The three constraints (6), (7), and (8) collectively say that when assigned to server j, task i should be completed no later than its deadline (i.e., the maximum allowed latency L_i). Task i's total delay on server j is given by $x_{ij}d_{ij} + \sum_{k=1}^{i-1} q_{ijk}d_{kj}$, as shown in (6) [14]. The two constraints (7) and (8) indicate that q_{ijk} is equivalent to $x_{ij}x_{kj}$. Note that (7) and (8) are called indicator constraints in CPLEX solver [15]. The $\sum_{k=1}^{i-1} q_{ijk}d_{kj}$ represents the queuing delay of task i if it is assigned to server j. Recall that the tasks are served in a first-come first-serve order. If task k arriving before task i (with $k \in \{1, \ldots, i-1\}$) is also assigned to server j, then task i has to wait till task k is finished. The queuing delay of task i on server j only makes sense when task i is assigned to server j. Therefore, (7) says that when task i is not assigned to server j, its queuing delay constraint (6) on server j should be removed [16].

To address the case of dynamic task arrival, we introduce an online greedy algorithm (shown as Algorithm 1) to be used by a system manager to maximize its total received revenue. The idea of the algorithm is: whenever a server is available, it should be given the task with the highest value among all tasks that are present in the system and can be completed before their deadlines by the server.

Algorithm 1. Online Greedy Task Distribution Algorithm

Require: $\langle \mathbb{N}_J(T), \mathbb{N}_S, T \rangle$, where T is the time period during which the algorithm executes, and $\mathbb{N}_J(T)$ is a set of tasks and their arrival times during T, and $\mathbb{N}_S$ is a server set.

1: $t \leftarrow 0$, $Q = \emptyset$ (Q is a priority queue where the task with the highest value is at the front of Q).

2: **while** $t \leq T$ **do**

3:     If a task arrives at time t, insert it into Q:

4:         If multiple tasks have the same value, order them according to their arrival time order.

5:         If a set of servers are available at time t (denoted by $\mathbb{S}_t \subseteq \mathbb{N}_S$), use a loop to select all servers one at a time and in random order from $\mathbb{S}_t$, and for each selected server svr_j:

6:             Start from the front of Q, search for the task with the highest value among all tasks that can be finished before their deadlines if processed by svr_j. Let $task^*$ denote such a task.

7:             If $task^*$ is found, stop search and start a new thread for svr_j to work on $task^*$.

8: **end while**

---

4   Performance Analysis

In this section comparisons have been drawn between existing and the proposed techniques in terms of energy consumption in joules and throughput analysis.

Between the proposed techniques and the some well known existing techniques. MATLAB 2013a tool has been used with the help of parallel processing toolbox to balance the load between HESs. The Computer used for the processing had standard configurations (Dell notebook computer with 8 GB RAM and 2.4 GHz Intel core i5 processor with 2 GPU built in). The proposed and other selected techniques (i.e., PSO (Wu et al. (2014)), Ant colony optimization (ACO), Multiobjective Variable Neighborhood Search (VNS) and Game Theory are implemented on the same experimental platform. Upto 4000 task have been tested on every technique. Following sections describes the comparison between proposed techniques with existing techniques.

Table 1 demonstrates the comparison between $MVNS$, ACO, PSO, Game Theory with Proposed technique based on energy consumption. A schedule is said to best if it has minimum energy consumption. Therefore, from the Table 1, it is observed that the proposed technique has minimum energy consumption. The mean reduction in the energy consumption is 0.42% when proposed technique is compared with other scheduling techniques.

Table 1. Energy consumption analysis of proposed technique

No. of tasks	MVNS [19]	ACO [70]	PSO [71]	Game theory [18]	Proposed
1000	1.33 ± 0.049	1.91 ± 0.078	0.98 ± 0.030	0.99 ± 0.038	0.98 ± 0.017
1500	1.98 ± 0.091	1.93 ± 0.089	0.94 ± 0.043	0.98 ± 0.049	0.91 ± 0.077
2000	1.89 ± 0.049	1.49 ± 0.080	0.89 ± 0.048	0.99 ± 0.081	0.87 ± 0.083
2500	1.98 ± 0.087	1.47 ± 0.083	1.93 ± 0.078	0.94 ± 0.048	0.90 ± 0.018
3000	1.97 ± 0.088	1.49 ± 0.097	1.38 ± 0.099	0.99 ± 0.041	0.89 ± 0.041
3500	1.84 ± 0.091	1.98 ± 0.098	1.78 ± 0.098	0.97 ± 0.098	0.91 ± 0.081
4000	1.99 ± 0.099	1.97 ± 0.087	1.98 ± 0.081	0.99 ± 0.099	0.78 ± 0.089

Table 2 demonstrates the comparison between $MVNS$, ACO, PSO, Game Theory with Proposed technique based on utilization. A schedule is said to best if it has maximum utilization. Therefore, from the Table 2, it is proved that the proposed technique has better utilization. The mean improvement in the efficiency is 0.5% when proposed technique is compared with other scheduling techniques.

Table 2. Utilization analysis of proposed technique

No. of tasks	MVNS [19]	ACO [70]	PSO [71]	Game theory [18]	Proposed
1000	0.73 ± 0.049	0.81 ± 0.078	0.78 ± 0.030	0.79 ± 0.038	0.92 ± 0.017
1500	0.78 ± 0.091	0.83 ± 0.089	0.94 ± 0.043	0.92 ± 0.049	0.96 ± 0.077
2000	0.89 ± 0.049	0.91 ± 0.080	0.93 ± 0.048	0.97 ± 0.081	0.98 ± 0.083
2500	0.78 ± 0.087	0.87 ± 0.083	0.83 ± 0.078	0.84 ± 0.048	0.89 ± 0.018
3000	0.77 ± 0.088	0.79 ± 0.097	0.83 ± 0.099	0.89 ± 0.041	0.92 ± 0.041
3500	0.84 ± 0.091	0.88 ± 0.098	0.89 ± 0.098	0.91 ± 0.098	0.94 ± 0.081
4000	0.79 ± 0.099	0.81 ± 0.087	0.91 ± 0.081	0.93 ± 0.099	0.95 ± 0.089

5   Conclusions and Future Work

In this paper, a novel game theoretic approach has been proposed to improve the throughput of the edge computing. Also, an effort is made to reduce the energy consumed during the offloading in the edge computing. In order to arrive at the successfulness of the proposed techniques, no. of tests have been conducted by considering the benchmark dataset. MATLAB 2013a tool has been used with the help of the parallel processing toolbox to offload the data in edge computing. The Dell notebook computer has been utilized with 8 GB RAM with 2.4 GHz Intel core i5 processor with 2 GB GPU built in. The proposed and existing techniques have been implemented on the same experimental platform. Upto 4000 jobs have been tested on every technique.

References

1. Yao, F., Demers, A., Shenker, S.: A scheduling model for reduced CPU energy. In: 1995 Proceedings of the Symposium on Foundations of Computer Science, pp. 374–382. IEEE, December 1995
2. Palacin, M.R.: Recent advances in rechargeable battery materials: a chemists perspective. Chem. Soc. Rev. **38**(9), 2565–2575 (2009)
3. Chen, X., Jiao, L., Li, W., Fu, X.: Efficient mutli-user computation offloading for mobile-edge computing. IEEE/ACM Trans. Netw. **24**(5), 2795–2808 (2016)
4. Mao, Y., You, C., Zhang, J., Huang, K., Letaief, K.B.: A survey on mobile edge computing: the communication perspective. IEEE Commun. Surv. Tutor. **19**(4), 2322–2358 (2017)
5. Satyanarayanan, M., Bahl, P., Caceres, R., Davies, N.: The case for VM-based cloudlets in mobile computing. IEEE Pervasive Comput. **8**(4), 14–23 (2009)
6. ETSI: Mobile-edge computing introductory technical white paper, White Paper, Mobile-edge Computing Industry Initiative (2015). https://portal.etsi.org/portals/0/tbpages/mec/docs/mobile-edgecomputing-introductorytechnicalwhitepaperv1
7. Chiang, M., Ha, S., Chih-Lin, I., Risso, F., Zhang, T.: Clarifying fog computing and networking: 10 questions and answers. IEEE Commun. Mag. **55**(4), 18–20 (2017)
8. Chen, M.-H., Liang, B., Dong, M.: A semidefinite relaxation approach to mobile could offloading with computing access point. In: Proceedings of the IEEE International Workshop on Signal Processing Advances in Wireless Communications (SPAWC), pp. 186–190, June 2015
9. Chen, M.-H., Liang, B., Dong, M.: Joint offloading decision and resource allocation for multi-user multi-task mobile cloud. In: Proceedings of the IEEE International Conference on Communications (ICC), pp. 1–6, May 2016
10. Cheng, J., Shi, Y., Bai, B., Chen, W.: Computation offloading in cloud-RAN based mobile cloud computing system. In: IEEE International Conference on Communications, pp. 1–6, May 2016
11. Yu, Y., Zhang, J., Letaief, K.B.: Joint subcarrier and CPU time allocation for mobile edge computing. In: Proceedings of IEEE GLOBECOM, pp. 1–6, December 2016
12. Wang, X., Wang, J., Wang, X., Chen, X.: Energy and delay tradeoff for application offloading in mobile cloud computing. IEEE Syst. J. **11**(2), 858–867 (2017)

13. Dinh, T.Q., Tang, J., La, Q.D., Quek, T.Q.S.: Offloading in mobile edge computing: task allocation and computational frequency scaling. IEEE Trans. Commun. **65**(8), 3571–3584 (2017)
14. You, C., Huang, K., Chae, H., Kim, B.-H.: Energy-efficient resource allocation for mobile-edge computation offloading. IEEE Trans. Wirel. Commun. **16**(3), 1397–1411 (2017)
15. Wang, Y., Sheng, M., Wang, X., Li, J.: Mobile-edge computing: partial computation offloading using dynamic voltage scaling. IEEE Trans. Commun. **64**(10), 4268–4282 (2016)
16. Cao, X., Wang, F., Xu, J., Zhang, R., Cui, S.: Joint computation and communication cooperation for mobile edge computing. arXiv:1704.06777 (2017)
17. Al-Shuwaili, A., Simeone, O., Bagheri, A., Scutari, G.: Joint uplink/downlink optimization for backhaul-limited mobile cloud computing with user scheduling. IEEE Trans. Sig. Inf. Process. Over Netw. **3**(4), 787–802 (2017)

Secure and Efficient Enhanced Sharing of Data Over Cloud Using Attribute Based Encryption with Hash Functions

Prabhleen Singh[1](✉) and Kulwinder Kaur[2](✉)

[1] Department of Computer Science and Information Technology,
Guru Nanak Khalsa College, Sultanpur Lodhi, Punjab, India
prabh_l@yahoo.com
[2] Department of Computer Science and Engineering, Jalandhar, Punjab, India
kulwinder.kaur0117@gmail.com

Abstract. Cloud computing is a model on which association and people can work with application from anywhere on demand. The real issue of cloud computing is preserving integrity and confidentiality of data in data security. The essential solution for this issue is data encryption on cloud. Security in cloud computing being one of the great research subjects. Numerous strategies have been proposed on attribute-based encryption systems. Attribute Based Encryption (ABE) is a cryptographic crude that understands the thought of cryptographic access control. This research work proposed attribute-based encryption method based on hash function associated with asymmetric encryption. The performance of the proposed algorithm has been evaluated by simulation using Cloudsim toolkit. For simulation we have analyzed the results on the basis of different File Size and simulated the results of proposed algorithm. Encryption Time, Key Generation Time and decryption time are evaluated and compared with the existing algorithm. Performance of proposed hash-based ABE algorithm is compared with the existing ABE algorithm. Experimental results demonstrate that proposed technique takes less time for encryption, decryption and for computing key than the existing technique and hence, performs better than existing algorithm. The average improvement is 13.54% in the proposed ABE with hashing as compared to existing ABE on the basis of encryption time; average approximate increase in the efficiency of key computation time is 3.72% as compared with the existing; 11.08% of improvement in decryption time.

Keywords: Cloud computing · Security · Data encryption
Attribute-based encryption

1 Introduction

With the growth of social networking sites and information technology, many people want to share important moments of their life on internet. Also, people may share various pictures consisting more private information about their family and friends

© Springer Nature Switzerland AG 2018
I. Traore et al. (Eds.): ISDDC 2018, LNCS 11317, pp. 102–117, 2018.
https://doi.org/10.1007/978-3-030-03712-3_9

using storage services of cloud like Google Drive and icloud. Users of internet trust cloud service providers that they protect their private data to avoid unauthorized access [9]. However, still some malicious users exploit vulnerability of system so that they access data on cloud to steal private information of users.

The rapid growth of information technology and communication encouraged incredible change in computational model, and directly lead to emergence and development of cloud computing. Cloud computing is executed based on concept of parallel computing, distributed computing, grid computing and so on. It is an item that integrates network techniques and conventional computing. It has various characteristics like ease of use, scalable, flexible, multiple network access, independent of location, economical and reliable [4].

Moreover, with rapid development of computer technology and internet, data on the network integrates exponentially and thus storage demand increases. Current conventional models for storage cannot handle this issue, and they have some problems to deal with enormous amount of data and devices connected by increasing business cost. Cloud storage is a internet based online storage system that uses concept of cloud computing and data of users are stored in various virtual servers provided by third party instead of their own servers. Normally, cloud service providers provide service of cloud storage by various storage servers with large amount of space for storage. Users can buy or rent space for storage from cloud service providers to meet their data storage requirements. For the concern of users, cloud storage does not allude to a particular storage gadget, however an accumulation of countless gadgets and servers [4]. The client isn't utilizing a particular storage gadget when he utilizes the services of cloud storage, however utilizes the services of information access brought by the cloud storage framework. In this way, entirely, cloud storage isn't just a storage, yet additionally a sort of service. The center of the cloud storage framework is a natural combination of an application programming and storage gadgets which has changed the situation from the basic storage gadgets to the cloud storage benefits by applying the application programming. In cloud storage benefits, the clients neither one of the needs to understand the sort, interfaces, storage media, and so forth, of the storage gadgets, nor require to oversee or keep up the capacity gadgets, for example, backup and disaster recovery activities. They can appreciate the distributed storage administrations without worry for the way of information storage by basically getting to distributed storage frameworks. It has not just successfully tackled the issues existing in conventional storage mode, yet in addition achieved extraordinary convenience to the clients. Contrasted with conventional storage modes, cloud storage mode has numerous points of interest: (1) Easier to development: cloud storage engineering embraces parallel extension, when the limit isn't sufficient, the cloud storage supplier simply need to buy new capacity servers, and the limit increments quickly and nearly without confinement; (2) Easy to manage: when the greater part of the information is relocated to the cloud storage, all the enhancement and upkeep assignments are finished by the cloud service provider and frees the framework director of the undertaking from the unpredictable administration assignments; (3) Lower cost: for moving huge amount of data to the distributed storage framework, enterprises require not to contribute much cash to purchase storage hardware and programming, however just require to purchase or lease storage space from the distributed storage suppliers, which decreases the cost of information storage; (4) Customized: distributed storage specialist organizations can give customized distributed storage benefit answers for a particular undertaking client, it not just gives the excellent individual benefit for business clients, yet additionally diminishes the security dangers to a specific degree. Due to previously mentioned favourable circumstances of distributed storage, an ever-increasing number of organizations have developed the distributed storage stages to give distributed storage administrations to big business or singular clients. The conventional cloud storage applications consist Amazon S3, Google Drive and, Microsoft's Windows Azure. Despite the fact that distributed storage has numerous points of interest, its advancement process is moderate. As indicated by the review give an account of distributed storage did by Twinstrata [1], just around 20% of clients will store their private information in the cloud storage framework, while almost 50% of respondents will utilize distributed storage administrations for information offsite reinforcement, documenting, catastrophe recuperation and different capacities. As indicated by the report, the security of distributed storage benefit is the most vital motivation behind why individuals don't depend on this glorious storage administration. Clearly, the security issue in cloud storage framework is one of the greatest hindrances in the improvement and advancement of cloud storage administrations. Just if the security issues of the cloud storage framework are very much comprehended, it will pick up fame and will add to the improvement of social monetary structure of the society by making lives of the general population more convenient.

Basic security concerns in cloud storage are portrayed in Fig. 1, which features the significant issues in cloud information security, i.e., information protection, accessibility and integrity. Specifically, cloud models won't not be adequately shielded from inside attacks. In virtual situations, amalicious client may have the capacity to break into "neighboring" virtual machines situated on a similar equipment and after that take, adjust or erase the other clients' information [14–20]. In such conditions, clients are in reality normally conceded with superuser access for dealing with their virtual machines. A malicious superuser can get to genuine system segments and in this way dispatch attacks [14, 21]. In addition, virtualization permits the rollback of a virtual machine to some past state if vital. In spite of the fact that this rollback include gives adaptability to the clients, it can likewise return the virtual machine to past security approaches and setup control [14, 16]. In the long run, virtual machine movement is rushed to enhance service quality. During such movement forms, which regularly do not close down administrations, virtual machine substance is uncovered to the system, and issues, for example, arrange exchange bottlenecks furthermore, damage to data may happen [14, 16, 22].

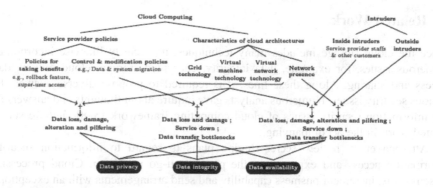

Fig. 1. Data security issues [2]

Traditional data security approaches, i.e., information encryption [23, 24], information anonymization [25], replication [26], information confirmation [27], information partition [28–30] and differential protection [34], can solve most data security issues inside cloud processing conditions (Fig. 2), yet generally each one in turn. Numerous information driven cloud applications don't just require information to be secure, yet additionally effectively gotten to, once in a while through difficult, scientific questions likened to online analysis processing (OLAP) activities. With clients looking to lessen costs in the cloud's pay-as-you-go evaluating model, accomplishing the best exchange off between data security and access control and proficiency is an incredible test [31, 32].

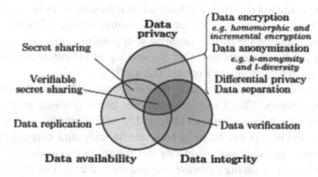

Fig. 2. Features of data security techniques [2]

The rest of the parts of this paper are organized as underneath: In Sect. 2, we audit a few related works about security systems for cloud storage. Section 3 presents basic encryption algorithm and attribute-based encryption, proposed work is presented in Sects. 4 and 5, Sect. 6 presents results and discussion and finally, Sect. 7 concludes the paper and presents future scope for this work.

2 Related Work

Since the cloud storage includes many techniques, its security likewise incorporates numerous issues, for example, data integrity, encrypted storage, cloud review, data access and sharing. Along these lines, it is required to propose diverse answers for various security issues. Numerous analysts gave inquire about thoughts and answers for the information security issues of cloud computing framework [5–8], and we survey related work in the accompanying.

Attasena et al. review secret sharing plans to regard to information security, information access and expenses in the pay-as-you-go paradigm. Cloud processing lessens costs, increment business capability and send arrangements with an exceptional yield on venture for some sorts of uses. In any case, information security is of premium significance to numerous clients and frequently limits their reception of cloud advancements. Different approaches, i.e., information encryption, replication and verification, help implement diverse aspects of information security. Secret sharing is an especially fascinating cryptographic system. Its most developed variations without a doubt at the same time authorize information security, accessibility and trustworthiness, while permitting calculation on encrypted information [2].

Casassa-Mont et al. particularly center around a cloud situation since it gives a rich arrangement of utilization cases including cooperations and data sharing among various partners, counting clients and service providers. Web communications for the most part require the trade of individual and secret data for an assortment of purposes, counting empowering business exchanges and the provisioning of administrations. A key issue influencing these communications is the absence of trust and control on how information will be utilized and handled by the substances that get it. In the conventional world, this issue is tended to utilizing authoritative agreements, those are marked by the included collections, and law requirement. This should be possible electronically also however, notwithstanding the trust issue, there is at present a noteworthy hole between the meaning of lawful contracts directing the sharing of information, and the product framework required to support and uphold them [3].

Li et al. consider the protected information access and sharing issues for cloud capacity administrations. Cloud storage is another capacity mode rose alongside the improvement of cloud computing worldview. By relocating the information to distributed storage, the buyers can be freed from the building and keeping up the private storage foundation, and they can appreciate the information storage administration at anyplace and whenever with high unwavering quality and a moderately ease. Be that as it may, the security and protection dangers, particularly the privacy and honesty of information appear to be the greatest obstacle to the selection of the distributed storage applications. In view of the unmanageability of the discrete logarithm issue, authors plan a secure information access and information sharing plan for distributed storage, where they use the client confirmation plan to manage the information get to issue. As per their investigation, through the plan, just substantial client with the right secret word and biometric can access to the distributed storage supplier. Also, the approved clients can get to the legitimate resources [4].

Florence et al. proposed a novel access control structure called as client utilization construct encryption developed in light of the accessible ascribe based encryption to ensure the information assurance. Utilization is mapped as accreditation with a period edge to each private quality. The information client can decipher a strengthened quality just if there is a match between the certifications related with the quality. Utilizing the component extraction calculation, the accessible encryption plot empowers a steady routing of encoded qualities. Multi-Credential routing is connected to fortify the privacy of the delicate records. Authors enable the information client to propagate the qualifications as per their use criteria likewise the client gets the keys as names alongside the credentials. The information proprietor will have the capacity to relate each enciphered attribute with an arrangement of accreditations [5].

Chen et al. proposed cloud-based secure transmission system which is appropriate for various clients. Electronic medical records containing confidential information were transferred to the cloud. The cloud permits medicinal groups to get to and deal with the information and combination of restorative records effortlessly. This information framework gives important data to the restorative workforce and encourages and improve electronic medical record administration and information transmission. A structure of cloud based also, patient-centered personal health record (PHR) is proposed in this study. This method helps patients to manage their wellbeing data, for example, arrangement date with specialist, wellbeing reports, and their very own finished comprehension wellbeing conditions. It will make patients inspirational states of mind to keep up the health. The patients make choice all alone for those whom approaches their records over a particular traverse of time indicated by the patients. Putting away information in the cloud condition can diminish expenses and improve the offer of data, however the potential risk of data security ought to be thought about [6].

Hong et al. receive multi-party calculation to figure it out security protecting total calculation in which at any rate t cloud servers can together figure the total outcomes without increasing any information of sensitive information. Outsourcing information to the cloud turns into a pattern for the clients to lessen database administration and support cost. In any case, putting away information on the cloud brings numerous security issues. Information protection and inquiry verification are two basic issues to be settled. Exceptionally, they are essential to total inquiries of cloud information. The information proprietor must keep the sensitive information covered up and just the total outcome is uncovered to the customers and cloud specialist organization. Besides, the customer can guarantee that the total outcomes are right and complete. In expansion, authors present a verified structure, called PAAT, to give question validation for total outcome. The test comes about demonstrate that this plan is practical and has great execution in practice [7].

Wei et al. proposed forward and backward secure CPABE to conquer practical issues of key presentation and client repudiation, while applying ABE to distributed storage frameworks. Particularly, authors first formally characterized the security thought, and after that gave a point by point development. This forward and backward secure CP-ABE conspire is demonstrated specifically secure in the standard model under a q-type multifaceted nature suspicion. The execution talk shows that the proposed plot outperforms other related ABE conspires as far as down to earth security ensures. In this manner, it is more attractive for securing cloud storage frameworks [8].

Wu et al. propose an incorporated plan including invisible watermarking, veiling and secret sharing strategies. The histogram adjustment-based plan can accomplish reversible information covering up to guarantee the honesty and classification of picture information. Furthermore, a secret sharing plan was utilized to additionally enhance the security of information access. The assessment outcomes demonstrate that the proposed framework may keep malicious clients from getting to private pictures [9].

Fan et al. proposed a distributed security control convention demonstrate with highlights of adaptable authorizing, include authoritative, and disconnected controlling. At long last, through the security appraisal of the convention and the execution investigation and reproduction, it has been demonstrated that the MUCON convention is compelling, secure, dependable, and effectively executed. Use control isn't just an old point yet in addition another test as the key innovation in framework security. With the improvement of cloud processing innovation, the clients' information assurance of cloud condition has turned into a hot zone of study. On account of the progression and multifaceted nature of cloud processing condition, get to control has turned into a more troublesome task, and it will get to an ever-increasing extent consideration from the specialists and ventures [10].

Fernandes et al. reviews the works on cloud security issues, making an exhaustive survey of the writing regarding the matter. It tends to a few key themes, to be specific vulnerabilities, dangers, and attacks, proposing a scientific classification for their grouping. It likewise contains a careful survey of the principle ideas concerning the security condition of cloud situations and, talks about a few open research points [11].

3 Basic Encryption Algorithm

Encryption algorithm [5] plays a significant part to build up a protected and classified correspondence over the system. It is the essential instrument for the protection of data. "The key" in the Enciphering algorithm changes the data to the scrambled frame. The general kinds of encryption algorithms are:

1. Symmetric Key Encryption: One secret key is utilized for both encryption and decryption. DES, 3DES, AES and RC4are the much of the time utilized symmetric encryption strategies. The symmetric calculation is of two types:
   (a) Block Cipher Symmetric Key Encryption: In this encryption, entire block is given as input. Examples are AES and DES.
   (b) Stream Cipher Symmetric Key Encryption: This encryption encrypts a single bit at a time. RC4 is an example of this encryption.
2. Asymmetric Key Encryption: It is a public key cryptosystem and utilizes a key match - a public key known to everyone, a private key known just to the recipient. Example consists of RSA algorithm.
3. Homomorphic Encryption: Homomorphic encryption performs operations on ciphertext. It can further have classified into two types:

(a) Partially Homomorphic: Just multiplication or addition activity can be done on ciphertext e.g. Pallier (added substance) and RSA (multiplicative) cryptosystem.
(b) Fully Homomorphic: Various effective evaluations are done on ciphertext such as Gentry's cryptosystem.

Encryption techniques require sharing secret key among the commuters to ensure secure interaction among users. But it is sometimes risky to share their private keys. Hence, in 1979, Adi Shamir introduced a cryptographic system in which any two clients can have a safe collaboration likewise confirm each other's signature without exchanging their public and private keys [5]. They don't depend on the third-party cloud service providers.

Again in 1984, he developed and implemented identity-based cryptosystem. It is public key framework based on email-address. The public string could incorporate a physical IP address or a domain name. The Identity based encryption (IBE) permits the client to create a public key from a known identity esteem such as an ASCII string.

In a typical public key cryptosystem, the message is enciphered utilizing people in public key of the receiver. In the ABE method with an arrangement of graphic traits the figure content &, the keys are marked. The message can be unscrambled just if there is a match between the properties of the cipher text and the properties of the client. The idea of Attribute Based Encryption was first proposed by Sahai and Waters [13] later adjusted by Vipul Goyal, Omkant Pandey, Amit Sahai and BrentWaters. Let us consider an example of conversation between two people.

4 Classification of ABE Attribute Based Encryption

The encryption is defined as conversion of data into non-readable form that can't be understand by human i.e. encoding. The conversion of encoding data into the readable format is known as decryption. Only the authorized person can have access to the key to decrypt the data. Thus, the data confidentiality is achieved by encryption. There are many encryption algorithms defined in the section above and each has its own advantages. In this paper, attribute-based encryption is a proven algorithm for cloud computing environment. The limitations of ABE methods are to be analyzed. ABE involves encrypting the attributes not the whole data. Encryption in this case is ease, secure and inexpensive as compare to other encryption methods discussed in the section above. ABE is secure encryption technique as it contains encrypted data in the form of attributes rather than the data itself. The data never leaked in any case of malicious attack. The limitation of this encryption is decryption is expensive. The performance of ABE is high as compare to other encryption algorithms. The below mentioned figure shows the classification of ABE.

In the normal public key encryption-based cryptosystem, the secret message is encrypted using the public key of the receiver side. In ABE, the encrypted text and the keys are labelled with the set of descriptive attributes. The decryption can be done only if the match between the attribute of cipher text and the attributes of the user.

The trusted party generates the encryption and decryption keys for the data owners and receivers. Public and master keys are generated by a complete set of pre-defined attributes.

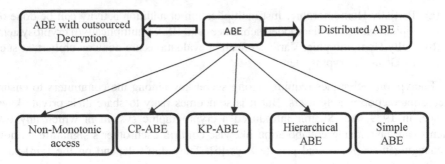

Fig. 3. Classification of attribute-based encryption

If a new attribute is added then new public and master keys are generated. The owner of the data encrypts the data with the public key and some attributes. The user receives the data can decrypt it using his own private key provided by the t rusted party. The attributes of the user's private key and attributes of the encrypted data are verified (Fig. 3).

If the number of matched attributes exceeds a predetermined threshold d, the user can decrypt the data using the private key. Otherwise, data can never be decrypted. Consider a simple example. Let the attributes be: "HOD", "Principal", "Secretary", "Professor", "Assistant Professor"," and "Guest Lecture". If the user is a staff, he has the attributes" Assistant Professor "and "Guest Lecture". If the HOD encrypts the file with attributes "Professor" and ("Assistant Professor" or "Guest Lecture") the staff will not be able to decrypt the data. If the attributes of the staff were "Assistant Professor" and ("Guest Lecture" or" Professor), he would have been able to decrypt the data.

5 Proposed Hash-Based ABE Algorithm

The proposed ABE algorithm contains the ABE with hash function associated with asymmetric encryption. To understand the concept of the proposed algorithm, some preliminaries needs to be studied. Basic concepts like Bi-linearity, non-degeneracy and Digital signature and has functions.

Access Structures: The access structure controlled the access rights that needs to be provided to users. It specifies the controlled access to the legitimate users. It provides the different access structure based upon the user's role and attributes.

An access structure $AS \subseteq 2^{B_1, B_2, B_3, B_4 \ldots \ldots B_n}$ is said to be known as monotone if $\forall$ D, C: $D \in AS$ and $D \subseteq C$ then $C \in AS$. An access structure AS is a set of non-empty subsets $B_1, B_2, B_3, B_4 \ldots \ldots B_n$ i.e. $AS \subseteq 2^{B_1, B_2, B_3, B_4 \ldots \ldots B_n} \backslash \emptyset$. Users with a set of attributes that are included in the AS are allowed access to the data. Sets do not belong to the AS are unauthorized sets of attributes. The ABE in its original form is limited monotone access structure.

Monotonic Access Structure: When an access structure S *is* satisfied by a set of attributes AS *then* any, A' where $AS \subseteq A'$ also satisfies S. The set in A' is called authorized sets otherwise it is unauthorized set. The original message has been partitioned to cqual size in order to efficiently encrypt the data.

Setup (λ, U, S): The authentic user setup the procedure considering lamda security parameter, U as universal description $U = \{1, 2, 3, 4. \ldots \ldots n\}$. The $\Phi(\lambda)$ generates output (pr, D, Dt, e) where D and Dt are the cyclic groups of prime order pr.

∀ attribute Ǝ i in 'U' ∀ i Ɛ U Ǝ "mk" Ɛ group G. There belongs a mapping between the group D elements that produce elements of Group Dt i.e. $D*D \rightarrow D_t$ [14]. Thus, the master key, public key and private key is generated.

Keygen (PK/MK/): The entire encryption process depends upon the key generation phase. This Keygen phase takes care of the assembling the keys required for the encryption and decryption operations.

Consider the vectors $\vec{Vi}$ $\vec{Vj}, \ldots \ldots \vec{Vn} \in Zp$ where Zp is a cyclic group.

The master key will be generated with the input of the asymmetric key public key.

Public key—From the fixed set Zp the reliable party arbitrarily chooses $t_1, t_2, t_3 \ldots \ldots \ldots \ldots t_n, y$. The public key PK is generated as

$PK = (t_1 = bt_1 \ldots \ldots \ldots \ldots \ldots, t_n = bt_n, Y = e(b, b)^y = bt_n)$ where b is a bilinear group and is generated by prime order pr.

Master Key—The master $MK = (t_1 \ldots \ldots .t_n, y)$

Private Key—This procedure takes as an input a set of user attributes UA and generate a private key as an output. For every user U the legitimate or trusted parties generates the private key. An arbitrary polynomial p of degree $q - 1$ is selected so that $f(0) = y$.

The private key is $PR\ Key = (D_1 = g(f(i))/(t_i))\forall i \in UA)$

Encryption (PK, MK): Encryption process takes PK and MK i.e. public key and master key as an input. The cipher text is generated by a set of user attributes i.e. UA. The master key generated, H i.e. hash matches with the access tree then create an encryption hash function that will results into digital signature. The encryption will take place only if the encryption hash function matches with access structure AS otherwise it will return null. The output if encryption is to find the value of H(x) which is the resultant encryption. The proposed Security Model is shown in Fig. 4 below.

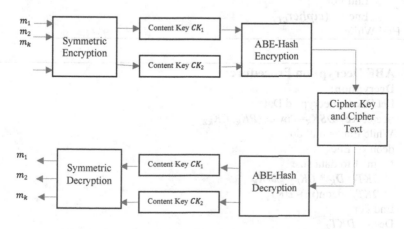

Fig. 4. Proposed attribute-based encryption with hashing

Decryption (PK, MK, AS, PR Key): The decryption takes public key, Access structure, master key and private key. The user can decrypt the text using the digital signature and private key. During the decryption process, If the set of attributes of cipher text matches the AS access structure to the user's private key, then the data can be decrypted. As the attributes of the cipher text matches with the attributes of the access structure the user can decrypt the data. The private key matches with the master key MK and access structure AS. The user with private key, if the private key of the user matches with the key present in the server then the hash function is decrypted otherwise it will return null. Decrypted hash function H(y) is verified with the initial generated hash function H(x).

The user is firstly authenticated with the public Key linked with the access structure AS. If the user is authenticated user then the secret key is generated and the private key contains key and the digital signatures also to enhance the security. Then the access id is assigned to the process. The access id linked with the user's private key and the secret key need to matched. The hashing is used for the mapping between the two sets. ABE encryption is hard to decrypt as proved by the existing ABE. In the proposed work, ABE structure is simplified by using hashing and digital signature.

ABE Encryption Procedure:
Let Da be the data to be encrypted
Let Enc be the encrypted Data
Private key PR_k ← generate key
Public Key PK_K ← generate random prime number
Master Key $MK = Power (C_{k1}, C_{k2})$ ← generate random even number less than public key
Secret Key SK_K ← (PR_k, C_{k2})
  while D != null do
     con ← D
  for k=1 to Size of Data
        $CipherT_1$=con(char(k)) + SK_K
        $CipherT_2$= $MK_{k1}*PK_K$
        $Cipher_{CT}$=$CipherT_1*CipherT_2$
    End For
    Enc ← ($cipher_{CT}$)
End While

ABE Decryption Procedure:
Decryption:
Let Dec be decrypted Data
Secret Key DSK_K=Power (PK_k, CK_{k2})
While Enc! =null do
dcon ← Enc
for m=1 to data size
  DKT_1=$D_K * CK_{k2} * MK_K$
  DKT_2=dcon(m)- DKT_1
End For
Dec ← DKT_2
End While

6   Results and Discussions

The performance of the proposed algorithm has been evaluated by simulation using Cloudsim toolkit. For simulation we have analyzed the results on the basis of different File Size and simulated the results of proposed algorithm. Encryption Time, Key Generation Time and decryption time are evaluated and compared with the existing algorithm.

Performance Comparison

We compared the performance of proposed hash-based ABE algorithm with the existing ABE algorithm, the performance is compared based on 3 performance metrics viz Encryption Time, Key Computation time and Decryption Time. The performance is evaluated by taking 5 different scenarios of jobs; and the comparison is done based on Honey Bee optimization based hyper heuristic algorithm with the other heuristic algorithms.

Table 1. Showing the comparison results of existing ABE and proposed ABE with hashing on the basis of varying file size for encryption time and key generation time.

	Existing		Proposed	
File size in MB	Encryption time in milliseconds	Key computation time	Encryption time	Key computation time
10	15.6	0.09	9.65	0.07
20	25.0	0.15	13.8	0.11
30	31.4	0.18	20.6	0.13
40	39.7	0.19	29.86	0.15
50	46.5	0.26	37.64	0.21
100	79.6	0.29	60.36	0.25
500	300.7	0.32	269.45	0.30

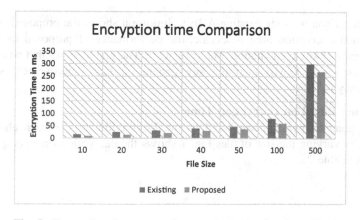

Fig. 5. Encryption time comparison on the basis of various file size

Performance Based on Encryption Time

In this section, the performance based on the Encryption time of each algorithm is compared by varying the size of files Fig. 5 shows the encryption time comparison of algorithms (Table 1).

The figure above shows the time taken to encrypt the data comparison based on different file sizes. The time of encryption is increasing as the file size increases. On comparison with the existing ABE technique it shows the proposed ABE with hash function encryption time is less i.e. the performance of proposed technique is better in terms of encryption parameter. The graph shows that when the file size increased to 500 MB then the encryption time improvement shown is approximately 10%.

Performance Based on Generation of Key Time

In this section, the performance based on the Key Computation time of each algorithm is compared by varying the size of files Fig. 6 shows the encryption time comparison of algorithms.

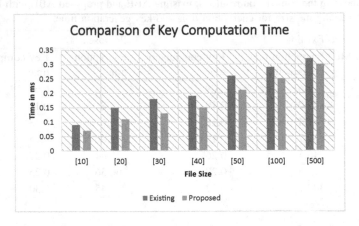

Fig. 6. Key Generation time comparison on the basis of various file size

On comparison with the existing ABE technique it shows the proposed ABE with hash function encryption time is less i.e. the performance of proposed technique is better in terms of key computation time parameter. The graph shows that when the file size increased to 500 MB then the key generation time improvement shown is approximately 6.25%.

Performance Based on Decryption Time

In this section, the performance based on the Decryption time of each algorithm is compared by varying the size of files Fig. 7 shows the decryption time comparison of algorithms (Table 2).

Table 2. Showing the comparison results of existing ABE and proposed ABE with hashing on the basis of varying file size for decryption time and key generation time

File size in MB	Existing		Proposed	
	Decryption time	Key computation time	Decryption time	Key computation time
10	10.2	0.09	7.22	0.07
20	15.7	0.15	11.8	0.11
30	21.6	0.18	19.8	0.13
40	29.3	0.19	25.6	0.15
50	36.6	0.26	32.8	0.21
100	59.8	0.29	45.9	0.25
500	150.4	0.32	102.9	0.30

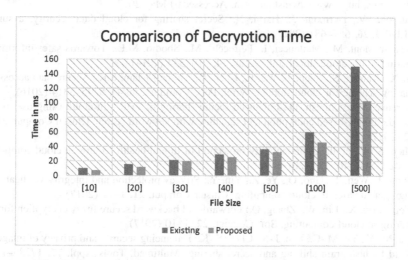

Fig. 7. Decryption time comparison on the basis of various file size

The figure above shows the time taken to decrypt the data comparison based on different file sizes. On comparison with the existing ABE technique it shows the proposed ABE with hash function decryption time is less i.e. the performance of proposed technique is better in terms of decryption parameter. The graph shows that when the file size increased to 500 MB then the encryption time improvement shown is approximately 31.5%.

7 Conclusion

Security in Cloud data storage is the major security issue. Many techniques are proposed to cover up this issue. When the level of security becomes increased then the confidentiality, integrity and privacy of the data will be more Hash function gives a better result for encryption. The present position Attribute Based Encryption for cloud computing has been discussed with its advantages. The proposed ABE based encryption algorithm with hash functions, digital signature and asymmetric encryption method. The existing ABE method is simplified sing the hash functions and will be suitable for the application that needs high level of security. The experimental results analyzed shows the encryption and decryption time reduction which indeed reflects in the of cost which is comparatively reduced. The average improvement is 13.54% in the proposed ABE with hashing as compared to existing ABE on the basis of encryption time; average approximate increase in the efficiency of key computation time is 3.72% as compared with the existing; 11.08% of improvement in decryption time.

References

1. Twinstrata. http://www.twinstrata.com. Accessed10 May 2012
2. Attasena, V., Darmont, J., Harbi, N.: Secret sharing for cloud data security: a survey. VLDB J. **26**, 657–681 (2017)
3. Casassa-Mont, M., Matteucci, I., Petrocchi, M., Sbodio, M.L.: Towards safer information sharing in the cloud. Int. J. Inf. Secur. **14**, 319–334 (2014)
4. Li, X., Kumari, S., Shen, J., Wu, F., Chen, C., Hafizul Islam, S.K.: Secure data access and sharing scheme for cloud storage. Wirel. Pers. Commun. **96**(4), 5295–5314 (2016)
5. Florence, M.L., Suresh, D.: Enhanced secure sharing of PHR's in cloud using user usage-based attribute-based encryption and signature with keyword search. Cluster Comput. **21**, 1–12 (2017)
6. Chen, S.-W., et al.: Confidentiality protection of digital health records in cloud computing. J. Med. Syst. **40**, 124 (2016)
7. Hong, J., Wen, T., Guo, Q., Ye, Z., Yin, Y.: Privacy protection and integrity verification of aggregate queries in cloud computing. Cluster Comput. **21**, 1–11 (2017)
8. Wei, J., Hu, X., Liu, W., Zhang, Q.: Forward and backward secure fuzzy encryption for data sharing in cloud computing. Soft Comput. **22**, 1–10 (2017)
9. Wu, M.-Y., Yu, M.-C., Leu, J.-S., Chen, S.-K.: Enhancing security and privacy of images on cloud by histogram shifting and secret sharing. Multimed. Tools Appl. **77**, 17285–17305 (2017)
10. Fan, K., Yao, X., Fan, X., Wang, Y., Chen, M.: A new usage control protocol for data protection of cloud environment. EURASIP J. Inf. Secur. **12**, 1–7 (2016)
11. Fernandes, D.A.B., Soares, L.F.B., Gomes, J.V., Freire, M.M., Inácio, P.R.M.: Security issues in cloud environments: a survey. Int. J. Inf. Secur. **13**, 113–170 (2013)
12. Florence, L., Suresh, D.: Cloud security and DES algorithm a Review. Int. J. Comput. Intell. Inf. **5**(2) (2015)
13. Sahai, A., Waters, B.: Fuzzy identity-based encryption. In: Cramer, R. (ed.) EUROCRYPT 2005. LNCS, vol. 3494, pp. 457–473. Springer, Heidelberg (2005). https://doi.org/10.1007/11426639_27
14. Ali, M., Khan, S.U., Vasilakos, A.V.: Security in cloud computing: opportunities and challenges. Inf. Sci. **305**, 357–383 (2015)
15. Derbeko, P., Dolev, S., Gudes, E., Sharma, S.: Security and privacy aspects in mapreduce on clouds: a survey. Comput. Sci. Rev. **20**, 1–28 (2016)
16. Hashizume, K., Rosado, D.G., Fernndez-Medina, E., Fernandez, E.B.: An analysis of security issues for cloud computing. Internet Serv. Appl. **4**, 1–13 (2013)

17. Joshi, J.B., Takabi, H., Ahn, G.J.: Security and privacy challenges in cloud computing environments. IEEE Secur. Priv. **8**, 24–31 (2010)
18. Khan, M.A.: A survey of security issues for cloud computing. J. Netw. Comput. Appl. **71**, 11–29 (2016)
19. Zhou, M., Zhang, R., Xie, W., Qian, W., Zhou, A.: Security and privacy in cloud computing: a survey. In: International Conference on Semantics, Knowledge and Grids, Beijing, China, pp. 105–112 (2010)
20. Zissis, D., Lekkas, D.: Addressing cloud computing security issues. Future Gen. Comput. Syst. **28**, 583–592 (2012)
21. Bilal, K., Malik, S.U.R., Khan, S.U., Zomaya, A.Y.: Trends and challenges in cloud datacenters. IEEE Cloud Comput. **1**, 10–20 (2014)
22. Zhang, F., Chen, H.: Security-preserving live migration of virtual machines in the cloud. Netw. Syst. Manag. **21**, 562–587 (2013)
23. Bellare, M., Goldreich, O., Goldwasser, S.: Incremental cryptography: the case of hashing and signing. In: Desmedt, Y.G. (ed.) CRYPTO 1994. LNCS, vol. 839, pp. 216–233. Springer, Heidelberg (1994). https://doi.org/10.1007/3-540-48658-5_22
24. Gentry, C.: Fully homomorphic encryption using ideal lattices. In: 41st Annual ACM Symposium on Theory of Computing, Bethesda, USA, pp. 169–178 (2009)
25. Cormode, G., Srivastava, D.: Anonymized data: generation, models, usage. In: 26th IEEE International Conference on Data Engineering, Long Beach, USA, pp. 1015–1018 (2010)
26. Padmanabhan, P., Gruenwald, L., Vallur, A., Atiquzzaman, M.: A survey of data replication techniques for mobile ad hoc network databases. VLDB J. **17**, 1143–1164 (2008)
27. Wang, Q., Wang, C., Li, J., Ren, K., Lou, W.: Enabling public verifiability and data dynamics for storage security in cloud computing. In: Backes, M., Ning, P. (eds.) ESORICS 2009. LNCS, vol. 5789, pp. 355–370. Springer, Heidelberg (2009). https://doi.org/10.1007/978-3-642-04444-1_22
28. Oktay, K.Y., Mehrotra, S., Khadilkar, V., Kantarcioglu, M.: SEMROD: secure and efficient mapreduce over hybrid clouds. In: International Conference on Management of Data (SIGMOD 2015), Melbourne, Australia, pp. 153–166 (2015)
29. Zhang, C., Chang, E.C., Yap, R.H.: Tagged-mapreduce: a general framework for secure computing with mixed-sensitivity data on hybrid clouds. In: International Symposium on Cluster, Cloud and Grid Computing (CCGrid 2014), Chicago, IL, USA, pp. 31–40 (2014)
30. Zhou, Z., Zhang, H., Du, X., Li, P., Yu, X.: Prometheus: privacy aware data retrieval on hybrid cloud. In: Proceedings of the IEEE, INFOCOM 2013, Turin, Italy, pp. 2643–2651 (2013)
31. Chow, R., et al.: Controlling data in the cloud: outsourcing computation without outsourcing control. In: 1st ACM Cloud Computing Security Workshop (CCSW 2009), Chicago, USA, pp. 85–90 (2009)
32. Sion, R.: Secure data outsourcing. In: 33rd International Conference on Very Large Data Bases (VLDB 2007), Vienna, Austria, pp. 1431–1432 (2007)

Blockchain Technology and Its Applications in FinTech

Wei Lu[1,2(✉)]

[1] Department of Computer Science, Keene State College, USNH, Durham, USA
wlu@unhlaw.unh.edu
[2] Peter T. Paul College of Business and Economics,
University of New Hampshire, Durham, NH, USA

Abstract. In this short paper we introduce the basics of blockchain technology including its many advantages and why and how they possess a number of attractive attributes for the banking and financial-services industry to simplify business processes while maintaining safe, trustworthy records of business agreement and transactions. In particular, some typical examples of applying blockchain in Financial Technology (FinTech) are discussed, including such as applying Bitcoin to drive various new business services, and implementing smart contracts based on blockchain technology to oversee the execution of legal transactions in real time. In addition, a pioneer effort of building up a distributed-ledger consortium model is addressed in the near future work.

1 Introduction

Blockchain is a technology to handle blocks in a chain. Each block including uniquely identified and linked transaction records is sealed cryptographically by a digital signature with a hash function based on the public key infrastructure (PKI). Such blocks are chained with each other in which the current block is connected to the previous block by referring its hash value, and thus the term blockchain is coined to represent the continuously growing, distributed and shared ledger of such blocks. The concept of blockchain is not new and its origins can be actually derived from technologies proposed decades ago [1] and it has gained its popularity with Bitcoin since 2008 when anonymous individual or group using a pseudonymous author named Satoshi Nakamoto introduced a white paper Bitcoin: A Peer-to-Peer Electronic Cash System [2].

The blockchain technology is essentially a general class of methods for decentralized records keeping of transactions and data sharing across multiple computing servers in a distributed fashion over different countries and institutions, leading two fundamental changes from trusting humans to trusting machines and from centralized control to decentralized control [3]. The computing servers, or nodes, connected to the blockchain verify if a transaction is valid or not based on the rules of governing logic known as smart contract. Once validation is confirmed, new records will be added to the ledger, recognized by all the nodes synchronously. Such a transaction can contain any type of data information including such as ownership of assets, digital identity, credit exposure, contractual obligations and even creative art copyrights.

© Springer Nature Switzerland AG 2018
I. Traore et al. (Eds.): ISDDC 2018, LNCS 11317, pp. 118–124, 2018.
https://doi.org/10.1007/978-3-030-03712-3_10

2   Blockchain and FinTech

The blockchain technology has recently gained attentions of the FinTech industry including such as major financial institutions, insurances agencies and the US Securities and Exchange Commission (SEC). Not only because of a large number of traded cryptocurrencies that are used in exchanges and transactions around the globe, the whole FinTech industry also cares more about referring the blockchain as a distributed ledger technology (DLT) and is allured by the two distinct opportunities provided behind the DLT, namely (1) utilizing the security, reliability and immutability of the underlying infrastructure, and (2) implementing the functionalities of smart contracts.

For FinTech, blockchain is a DLT in which all records in a shared, tamper-proof replicated ledger are made irreversible and nonrepudiable due to the one-way cryptographic hash function. Also an immutable historic transaction records between peers validated by community consensus generate a unique reconciled version of the truth in the system, and thus it becomes extremely difficult for an individual or a group to tamper with such a record, leading a mutual trust between peers. FinTech can re-build their bank-to-bank (B2B) transactions by implementing such a DLT platform to improve the performance such that an agreement could be reached in a very short time, compared to many centrally managed national systems that take typically one or several days between issuance and settlement.

Since DLT can record securely the transactions of anything that can be digitally represented, including such as fiat currency, arbitrary securities, and physical goods (e.g. gold and silver), it gives FinTech sector tremendous opportunities for building smart contracts to implement novel financial services securely so securities are traded and decomposed later without any manual oversight.

In summary DLT driven by blockchain technology "has the potential to reduce transaction latency, operational risk, process friction, liquidity requirement, and more" [4], and there are also many other new interesting applications arisen in the context of insurance, supply-chain monitoring and Internet of Things (IoT) based machine-to-machine (M2 M) communications. In the following we discuss two typical uses of blockchain in FinTech, namely Bitcoin [5] and Smart contract [6], and then address a pioneer effort of building up a distributed-ledger consortium model in the future work [7].

3   Bitcoin

Bitcoin is not only the first example of using blockchain technology and community validation, but also has a market capitalization of more than 115 billion as of July 2018 and remains the largest-scale application [8]. In the early stage of Bitcoin, it was de facto the only cash that was exchanged in the deep web accessed through ToR network [9], for example in between 2011 and 2013 the black market Silk Road operated in the deep web generated a revenue of about $3 billion by trading illegal services and goods underground [10]. Thanks to the increasing interests of practitioners, academics and the general public media attention, Bitcoin now has been used by various individuals as a medium of exchange in small businesses, leading more than 100,000 transactions a day based on statistics of Bitcoin Charts [11].

Hash is one of the most fundamental technologies used in Bitcoin and it is basically a mathematical operation to transform any size of digital information into a fixed size of bits, e.g. Secure Hash Algorithm (SHA 256) will produce 256-bit output numbers and SHA512 will produce 512-bit output numbers. There are two typical attributes of Hash, namely (1) Hash is irreversible that means it is impossible to re-construct the original message based on the output, and (2) in Hash any two very similar inputs will lead a completely different output. In cryptography Hash is usually considered as the fingerprint of the message (a.k.a. message digest). As illustrated in Fig. 1, the Hash function $H()$ takes as input an arbitrary length message and outputs a fixed-length string that is "message signature" in which $H()$ is a many-to-1 function and is often called a "hash function". As discussed above the desirable properties of $H()$ are: (1) it is easy to calculate and irreversibility, that is we cannot determine m from $H(m)$, and (2) it has collision resistance, that is it is computationally difficult to produce m and m' such that $H(m) = H(m')$ and seemingly random output. For example, as illustrated in Fig. 2, given plaintext *0000 0000 0000 0000* and key *2223 4512 987A BB23*, the output of Hash is *4789 FD47 6E82 A5F1*, we then change only one number in the first plaintext and have plaintext *0000 0000 0000 0001*. With the same key the output of Hash becomes to *0A4E D5C1 5A63 FEA3*. From this example we can see with only number changed in the plaintext, the outputs of the Hash would be totally different.

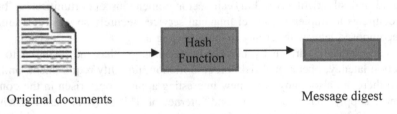

Original documents   Message digest

Fig. 1. Hash function

Plaintext:	Key:	Hash value:
0000 0000 0000 0000	22234512987ABB23	**4789FD476E82A5F1**
Plaintext:	Key:	Hash value:
0000 0000 0000 0001	22234512987ABB23	**0A4ED5C15A63FEA3**

Fig. 2. Hash value with two slightly different inputs

In the Bitcoin blockchain each block containing information such as previous block hash, time stamp, nonce, and transactions, will be hashed into a hash value of that block which is illustrated in Fig. 3 and then all the blocks are linked together through the consecutive hash numbers generated from the content of the previous block plus a random part which is illustrated in Fig. 4.

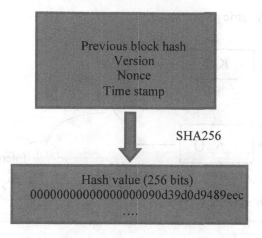

Fig. 3. Hash value of a block

The transaction of Bitcoin is as easy as sending an email using PGP protocol [12] and it requires three key elements, namely public key, private key and Bitcoin address. As illustrated in Fig. 5, suppose Alice wants to send a confidential e-mail, m, to Bob, what Alice would do in PGP include (1) generates random symmetric private key, K_S; (2) encrypts message with K_S; (3) also encrypts K_S with Bob's public key and (4) sends both $K_S(m)$ and $K_B(K_S)$ to Bob. After Bob received the PGP email, what Bob would do includes (1) uses his private key to decrypt and recover K_S and (2) uses K_S to decrypt $K_S(m)$ to recover m.

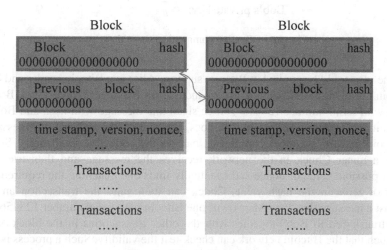

Fig. 4. Bitcoin blockchain

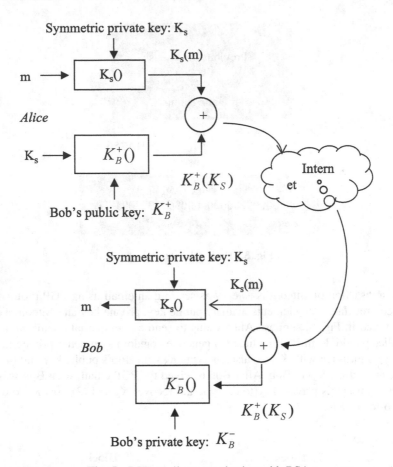

Fig. 5. PGP email communication with RSA

Same idea could be applied in Bitcoin, suppose Alice is a Bitcoin sender and Bob is a Bitcoin recipient, a transaction record includes a message "Alice gives Bob one Bitcoin with serial number 123456". Alice signs this message with hash and Bob then receives it and verifies if it is valid. If it does, Bob will then broadcast this message on the Bitcoin network so other participants can do the collective validations. Suppose there is a miner Chuck in the network receives the message and then tries many different possible value of nonce and eventually finds one matching the required initial number of zeros in the hash value, Chuck can then valid the transaction and later broadcast a message that "yes Alice owns one Bitcoin with serial number 123456 and it can be transferred to Bob" together with the other transactions in the block and the nonce such that the Bitcoin network can check-test the validity. Such a process is called Bitcoin mining.

4 Smart Contracts

Smart contracts, a term invented by Nick Szabo, is "a set of promises, specified in digital form, including protocols within which the parties perform on these promises." [13]. Smart contracts can be applied to execute automatically business workflows across multiple organizations. For example if we want to have a legal movement of physical goods from country A to country B, we typically need the import and export permissions from the two countries involved. To be granted permissions we also need to make sure tax/duties are cleared with evidence of payment which is required for permissions. In the meantime the vendors and buyers also need to cover finance gap before the receipt of payments or goods, and thus they may also buy insurances to cover their loss caused by risk. In this process many parties are involved including vendors, buyers of the goods, transporters, banks, insurance companies and customs departments of different countries. Such a process is called a workflow that could be managed by a sequence of computer programs that are run condition by condition to reach mutual goals defined in the smart contracts.

As illustrated in Fig. 6, smart contract is an implementation of natural language based contract in a fashion of computer code [14]. Considering such programs embody agreements between two or more organizations, the blockchain technology becomes a natural home for implementing smart contracts mainly because (1) in blockchain, all participants have common knowledge, making it impossible for one participant to plausibly repudiate a shared content at a subsequent time; (2) in blockchain the historical records are effectively immutable, and (3) each participant has a copy of the shared ledger and these copy stay in synchronization with one another, making it a significant challenge for one who wants to alter the shared contents.

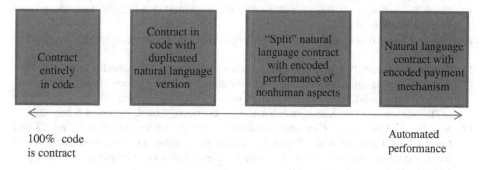

Fig. 6. Smart contracts, computer code versus natural language

5 Conclusions and Future Work

In this short paper we introduce blockchain basics and discuss how and why blockchain can be taken by the banking and financial-services industry to make significant impact on FinTech. A Distributed-Ledger Consortium Model, also known as Corda, has been conducted by R3 to adapt exiting DLTs to financial sectors through a global consortium including more than 80 financial institutional members [7]. For FinTech, the excitement of Corda is only matched by that for the emerging WWW in the middle of 1990s. In the near future we can expect the development of blockchain platform built from the ground up to address finance-specific needs, proof-of-concepts, pilot projects of applying blockchain to the new marketplace.

References

1. Merkle, R.C.: A digital signature based on a conventional encryption function. In: Pomerance, C. (ed.) CRYPTO 1987. LNCS, vol. 293, pp. 369–378. Springer, Heidelberg (1988). https://doi.org/10.1007/3-540-48184-2_32
2. Nakamoto, S.: Bitcoin: A Peer-to-Peer Electronic Cash System. Bitcoin (2008). https://bitcoin.org/bitcoin.pdf. Accessed 6 July 2018
3. The Trust Machine. The Economist, 31 October 2015. https://www.economist.com/leaders/2015/10/31/the-trust-machine. Accessed 6 July 2018
4. Hines, P., Dwyer, J.: Beyond the buzz: exploring distributed ledger technology use cases in capital markets and corporate banking. Technical report. CELENT and MISYS, August 2016. https://www.slideshare.net/BjornGeelhoed/beyond-the-buzz-blockchain-white-paper-by-celent-and-misys. Accessed 6 July 2018
5. Taylor, M.: The evolution of bitcoin hardware. IEEE Comput. 50(9), 58–66 (2017)
6. Magazzeni, D., McBurney, P., Nash, W.: Validation and verification of smart contracts: a research agenda. IEEE Comput. 50(9), 50–57 (2017)
7. Khan, C., Lewis, A., Rutland, E., Wan, C., Rutter, K., Thompson, C.: A distributed-ledger consortium model for collaborative innovation. IEEE Comput. 50(9), 29–37 (2017)
8. Marketcap with prices of cryptocurrencies like bitcoin and ethereum. CCN, 7 July 2018. https://www.ccn.com/marketcap/. Accessed 7 July 2018
9. Tor Project. Torproject, 7 July 2018. https://www.torproject.org/. Accessed 7 July 2018
10. Tasca, P., de Roure, C.: Bitcoin and the PPP Puzzle. SSRN, 2 July 2014. http://dx.doi.org/10.2139/ssrn.2461588
11. Bitcoin Charts. Blockchain, 8 July 2018. https://www.blockchain.com/charts. Accessed, 8 July 2018
12. OpenPGP. OpenPGP, 8 July 2018. https://www.openpgp.org/. Accessed 8 July 2018
13. Szabo, N.: Smart contracts: building blocks for digital markets. Extropy (1996). http://www.fon.hum.uva.nl/rob/Courses/InformationInSpeech/CDROM/Literature/LOTwinterschool2006/szabo.best.vwh.net/smart_contracts_2.html. Accessed 8 July 2018
14. Murphy, S., Cooper, C.: Can smart contracts be legally binding contracts? - an R3 and Norton Rose Fulbright White Paper. In: Norton Rose Fulbright, November 2016. http://www.nortonrosefulbright.com/files/r3-and-norton-rose-fulbright-white-paper-full-report-144581.pdf. Accessed 8 July 2018

Author Index

Alshanketi, Faisal   38
Awad, Ahmed   38

Bhatnagar, Shikhar   30
Butakov, Sergey   30

Dhurandher, Sanjay Kumar   16

Ibrishimova, Marina Danchovsky   50

Jaekel, Arunita   1

Kanan, Awos   38
Kaur, Amanjot   94
Kaur, Kulwinder   102
Kaur, Ramandeep   94

Li, Kin Fun   50
Lu, Wei   118

Malik, Yasir   30
Moritz, Stephan   74

Raniyal, Maninder Singh   16

Saad, Sherif   1
Saini, Ikjot   1
Singh, Prabhleen   102

Traoré, Issa   38

Uzunkol, Osmanbey   74

Wang, Zhiwei   63
Woungang, Isaac   16

Xie, Hao   63
Xu, Yumin   63